Conservation

Intext Series in ECOLOGY

ARTHUR S. BOUGHEY, *Editor*
University of California, Irvine

Conservation

Archie S. Mossman
Humboldt State University

Intext Educational Publishers
New York and London

Library of Congress Cataloging in Publication Data

Mossman, Archie Stanton, 1926–
    Conservation.

    (Intext series in ecology)
    Bibliography: p.
    1. Conservation of natural resources. I. Title.
S938.M67   333.7'2   73–16215
ISBN 0–7002–2446–7

Intext Educational Publishers
257 Park Avenue South
New York, New York 10010

Contents

Series Preface

As we move further into the 1970's we are confronted with dire threats of imminent environmental disaster. While prophecies as to the actual doomsday vary from five years to thirty years from now, no professional ecologist seems willing to state categorically that mankind will survive into the next millenium unchallenged by any ecocatastrophe. Some indeed believe that before this time we and most of our familiar ecosystems are inevitably doomed to extinction.

Enough has now been said and written about such predicted disasters to instill in students, governments, and the public at large an uneasy feeling that something may be amiss. Terms such as *pollution, natural increase,* and *re-cycling* have begun to assume a realistic and more personal note as the air over our cities darkens, our rivers are turned into lifeless fire hazards, our domestic water becomes undrinkable, and we have to stand in line for any form of service or amenity.

Politicians, scientists, and the public have responded variously to this new situation. Tokenism is rampant in thought, word, and deed. Well-intentioned eco-activist groups have mushroomed, not only among youth, who are the most threatened as well as the most understanding segment of our societies. More specifically, in the restricted field of college texts, appropriate ecological chapters have been hurriedly added to revised editions. No biological work is now permitted to conclude without some reference to human ecology and environmental crises.

The purpose of this new ecological series is to survey without undue overlap the major fields of our present environmental confrontation at an introductory college level. The basic text for the series presents an overview of the ecological fundamentals which are relevant to each issue. In association with the works listed in its bibliographical references, it can stand alone as a required text for an introductory college course. For such use each chapter has been provided with a set of review questions. For more extensive courses, the base text leads into each series volume, and the particular area of environmental problems which this explores.

This series treats, subject by subject, the main points of impact in this current ecological confrontation between man and his environment. It presents in breadth and in depth the problems of pollution, pesticides, waste materials, population control, and the resource exploitation which imminently threaten to overwhelm us. Each volume in the series is a definitive study prepared by a specialist in the field, writing from an intimate personal experience of his area, relating but not overlapping his subject with other volumes in the series. Uniquely assembled in each volume will be information which presently is not available without extensive bibliographical research, at the same time arranged and interpreted in a more readily assimilable form. Extensive illustrative material, much of it original, still further facilitates a ready comprehension of the matter presented.

This is an exciting series. The urgency and ferment which have been experienced by all those associated with it cannot fail to be transmitted to the reader. The series confounds the prophets of doom, for it illustrates that given a proper understanding of ourselves and our ecological world, there is yet time for action. This time may be short, but sufficient if we excerise now the characteristics of courage and resolution in which, at times of great crisis, our species has never previously been found wanting.

Arthur S. Boughey

Preface

       I have written this book to elaborate a thesis: That we are confronted by the need to make decisions about our planet that will have important ecological consequences and that there is no way of predicting outcomes with certainty. Therefore I advocate evaluating each problem within the broadest possible ecological context and choosing among options that action which will leave to future choice the greatest number and variety of acceptable new ecological options.

       Such a process cannot be exact. The reader will soon realize that much of the material presented here is of necessity hypothetical in nature and will expect, as I do, that some portions will prove erroneous. However, I hope the reader will pick up along the way not only facts but a way of thinking about conservation, and will begin the development of a benevolent personal conservation ethic.

       In preparing these chapters I have drawn upon my own experience not only to illustrate principles with specific cases but also because these were the experiences that enriched my own thinking about conservation and led to the generalizations expressed here.

       Conservation is only partly based on science, so this book is written as much for the nonscientist as for the scientist. I have attempted to emphasize social considerations in order to broaden the outlook of those specializing in science, and for the same reason I have tried to impress on nonscientists the essential role of science in conservation issues. Thus this text should be especially useful for introductory courses and useful for almost anyone who wishes to explore the complex considerations involved in conservation. It could also serve as an adjunct text for those ecology, geography, general biology, and environmental management courses that include the practical application of ecological principles.

I am greatly indebted to my colleagues, students, and many friends here and overseas who have helped me to gain conservation understanding, and also to my past teachers, especially my parents. My indebtedness to the authors of the literature that I have read is considerable. This source of insight probably surpasses all others in importance. J. M. Borgerson, G. F. Crandell, D. L. Hauxwell, R. L. Hurley, and F. H. Kilmer have made much appreciated contributions during preparation of the manuscript. W. C. Peters has provided several of his excellent black and white drawings for use in the body of the book. P. E. Palmquist prepared the photographic materials and K. McCutcheon, E. McClellan and D. B. Webb all assisted in preparing the manuscript. I am indebted to all of them. B. Allen and H. W. Grammelspacher helped considerably by reading all and part of the manuscript respectively. The reviewers have greatly improved this text, for which I am sincerely grateful. I especially want to express my appreciation to my wife Sue Y. Lee-Mossman who has helped me so much during all stages in the preparation of this text.

Introduction

Conservation is the physical and mental utilization (such as aesthetic appreciation) of resources (in the broadest sense) that leaves open or creates a maximum number and kind of possible uses for the future. No matter where one lives, he is confronted with conservation issues. Shall we have more industrial plants, or keep what recreational opportunities, open space, and clean air we have left? How much industry will we have before its advantages are masked and finally swamped by its disadvantages? Are we prepared to accept an occasional worm in an apple in order to avoid the toxic effects of DDT and DDE? Are we prepared to eliminate virtually all motorized private transportation from the more crowded areas of our medium- and large-sized cities to help solve air pollution and traffic congestion problems? Are we prepared to forego immediate profits from oil production in the Arctic so that the utilization of this resource can be achieved without damage to important ecological, social, and aesthetic assets? Are we prepared to use less electricity in order to reduce radioactive pollution, as well as pollution from the burning of coal and gas needed to produce it, and to avoid having to dam still more of our waterways?

The answer to such questions will soon have to be "yes" for many of us, especially in North America and Europe, because, barring the occurrence of high mortality in mankind, there will be no other alternative. The reasons are varied, and the situations in different areas of the world are strikingly dissimilar. Yet we *are* one world. We must all recognize at least our biological brotherhood if we, as a species, are to have meaningful lives and perhaps even if we are to survive. This leads to the second important understanding required for us to extricate ourselves from our conservation predicament, namely, the absolute necessity for a holistic approach, for "getting the big picture."

In the State University and College System of California, an employee requires a special license, in addition to his regular driver's license, if he drives state-owned vehicles. To obtain this license, it is necessary to view a motion picture which emphasizes some important rules for safe driving. Three of these are, "aim high," (look far down the road) "get the big picture," (keep aware of all sides and rear) and "leave yourself an out," (do not drive into a situation in which another's unexpected action makes you vulnerable). It has been noted that these three statements suggest how to survive in the academic profession. They also serve as a good recipe for human survival.

Our collective failure to use a holistic approach in decision making is as much to blame for our predicament as anything. We have cheered an increasing gross national product, the GNP, and have never considered it in terms of the losses involved. The GNP is a deceptive figure when it is used to measure the economic–environmental health of a nation. In order to produce all the goods and foodstuffs we consume each year, we sacrifice other things such as clean rivers, lakes, and oceans, clean air, outdoor recreational opportunities, aesthetically pleasing cities, our health, our life span, and so on. Thus the GNP, to be more meaningful, should have these items subtracted from it. They could collectively be called the gross national disproduct or GND, as suggested by Giles (1969). In addition, we live in a world with other people. Aerially sprayed DDT in Montana contaminates fish eaten in Moscow and Zurich. GNPs and GNDs still lack adequate adjustments for this type of environmental transgression.

Even if we choose to ignore such relationships in the interest of simplification, and so restrict ourselves within political boundaries, however large or small they may be, there are still further complexities which must be considered. Among the most important losses constituting part of the GND are aesthetic factors, and the removal of opportunities for sociological, ecological, and economic choices in the future. Our failure to "leave ourselves an out," that is, to maintain sociological, ecological, and economic options, may well become disastrous for us on a massive scale.

To extricate ourselves from the ecological noose that is rapidly tightening around our collective neck, much of the world population will very soon have to accept at least a reduction in amenities. Only those living in communities with resources, including energy, in surplus can do this. Those living at a subsistence level cannot. As a result, people having surplus resources also have power. This includes the power to concentrate more of the world's resources under their control, thus forcing more and more people into subsistence-level existence. The history both of man's tendency to do this and of the conflict between the underprivileged and the powerful is well known. It is almost certain that this will happen again unless those who control surplus resources share them with those who do not. And this applies on an international as well as on national and local levels.

Considerations such as these go beyond politics and economic organization. We are discussing matters of survival. Through the use of disease organisms, potent radiomimetic chemicals (chemicals that cause physiological changes similar to those induced by ionizing radiation), and so on, almost any country is large and powerful enough to strike a near-fatal blow to another country of almost any size. Thus an impoverished country could blackmail a rich country, forcing it to share its resources. Although this is an oversimplified statement of the problem of resource distribution and its possible consequences, the problem is a real one, and is one of the most important in the world today. The longer we delay confronting it, the less chance we will have of solving it (see page 11).

To solve our conservation problems we will have to approach them from a holistic viewpoint. This must include leaving ourselves as many environmental "outs" as possible, because we cannot confidently predict the world's future, especially now that we have so altered it. Our forefathers could claim with some truth that they left us this raped planet because they did not know better. That excuse is gone.

Options

1

CONSERVATION ETHICS

Conservation is everybody's business. If our lives can be described as *really* good, then good conservation is being practiced. We may not realize it, but many of the stresses we feel are caused by poor conservation. It has never been satisfactory to teach conservation only to those whose primary interests lie in the out-of-doors. Conservation must become everyone's way of life. Our mores should include recognition of the necessity for husbanding the earth. Leopold (1949) noted that in addition to our other ethics we require a "land ethic." Many of us already have it. We now need an ethic that encompasses the whole biosphere and even the space beyond our own planet, one that also takes into account long-range considerations, including posterity's right to optimum resources.

Civilization has been defined as ". . . social organization of high order, marked by the development of a written language and by advances in the arts, sciences, government, etc . . ." (Webster's New World Dictionary, 1970). One can certainly argue with this definition on several counts. Nowadays, the practice of conservation should certainly be included. That it is not probably results in large part from the egocentricity of mankind and our Judeo-Christian background [McHarg (1969), and for a somewhat different view, Moncrief (1970)].

Only if social pressure is brought to bear on those who demolish our bases for existence will there be a chance that man (*Homo sapiens*) can survive in the face of his own reproductive and technological potential. Many "savages" should be considered civilized because of their treatment of natural resources, although this does not mean that they cannot learn from more technologically advanced peoples.[1] However, *we* can learn a

---

[1]Unfortunately, they almost always seem to learn and practice our least desirable traits.

great deal from them, for they are ahead of us in the integration of their cultures with the environment.

In southern Africa, clan membership determines one's eating and matrimonial habits. A person of the Dube (zebra) clan, for example, may not eat zebra *(Equus burchelli)* meat and may not marry another member of his or her clan. An Athapaskan Indian group believes that wild animals allow themselves to be taken for food. As a token of respect and gratitude for this, whenever they make a kill certain parts of the animal are placed in the nearest flowing water as an offering.

A Tlingit Indian friend in Alaska told about some of her peoples attitudes toward wildlife. For example, "One should not swear at a wild animal. They have feelings just like the rest of us." In the hunting ritual in Germany to this day, the deer killed are laid on their right sides and a twig of oak or evergreen placed in their mouths as a last bite or last meal. They are honored in a special ceremony by a wood fire under the stars.

These attitudes and practices may well have resulted from sad experience. The massive extinction of large animals in Pleistocene times may have been largely the work of man (Martin, 1967). Perhaps a similar history lies behind the Chinese proverb, "Cheat the earth. Earth will cheat you."

We should think about how these practices help people to live in harmony with their environment. Then we should apply these lessons in solving our own environmental problems.

Complete mixing of the world's peoples and cultures would be very unfortunate. Some mixing is certainly not to be frowned upon, but it is the diversity of humans and societies that contributes much of the interest and excitement of our existence. Without the Tlingit culture, how could we so easily acquire the feeling that wild animals taken for our use merit respect? How could a person be a "game hog" if he had this as part of his ethical framework? Perhaps the most valuable feature of cultural diversity is that it provides the raw material from which necessary cultural innovations can be developed. Just as the oneness of all life is to be cherished, so is the richness of life's diversity. To deprecate either is to deprecate life.

If conservation is to become a reality, it must now be fitted into the larger complex of human existence, not just tacked onto the outside like a scrap of tar paper covering a knothole. For example, some people feel that we should preserve only small natural areas to be looked at in the future by those not so fortunate as ourselves. This has worked very poorly, and will work less effectively as time goes by. Small areas serving as natural museums are valuable, but alone are inadequate. With an increasing world population, unless the conserved remnants of natural areas are of sufficient size to serve their purpose and are made meaningful, at least to a powerful minority, they will be converted to other uses. Sociological and economic, as well as aesthetic and scientific aspects of conservation, must be integrated successfully into any scheme that is to have long-term success (Myers, 1972a, b).

INTERNATIONAL AID

Those who have responsibilities for the "development" of the "under-developed" countries have made many serious mistakes (Farvar and Milton, 1972). By operating in a simplistic manner and not concerning themselves with the wider implications of their actions, they have unwittingly caused great harm. A simplistic approach to development is especially devastating to the so-called "primitive societies," because all parts of these societies are very closely interdependent. The slightest change in one aspect reverberates throughout the whole structure of the society. This has been recognized by social anthropologists for many years. Rappaport (1967) mentions, for example, "The taboos operate . . . to direct most of the subsidiary . . . animal protein to two categories very much in need of them: women and children. . . . Like thermostats, rituals have a binary aspect . . . the rituals of the Tsembaga [of New Guinea] . . . [affect] the size of the pig population, the amount of land under cultivation, the amount of labor expended, the frequency of warfare, and other components of the system." Almost no one, from the missionaries of the past to the present U.S. Agency for International Development (AID), has bothered to listen to them and to plan accordingly. To illustrate this more specifically: A group concerned with international aid in South America realized that changes can cause cultural turmoil. Its members attempted to be very cautious by only persuading the local populace to replace their digging hoes with ox-drawn plow. A more drastic way to influence their lives is hard to imagine. The possible repercussions in terms of population increase alone and the strains this could put on land tenure systems are frightening. Such "advances" may be "good," *if* appropriate assistance can be given to every aspect of existence, and *if* the people themselves largely determine the directions and rates of development.

By single-minded yet well-intentioned approaches to specific problems, such as the AID effort to eliminate the tsetse fly (*Glossina* spp.) from Africa, we set in motion inevitable ecological and social processes which can drastically reduce the ability of a continent to support mankind (Mossman, 1966). We need instead multidimensional approaches to the assistance of developing countries, and it is important that the citizens of these countries have the major roles in planning and implementing assistance programs. We can no longer tolerate simple goals such as the elimination of malaria or of tsetse flies, or the promotion of the wool-growing industry, unless it is first agreed that good conservation must prevail. As soon as this has been agreed, ecological tunnel vision is impossible. Without such agreement, more harm than good commonly results.

Conservation is a responsibility of the big-city slum dweller just as it is of the commercial fisherman or of a country's rulers. The ghetto dweller has an especially difficult road ahead, but in his battles to end ghetto life, he will be fighting for conservation. We are all in the worldwide conservation predicament together, whether we like it or not. I am increasingly optimistic that we will extricate ourselves by cooperative effort before it is too late. If we succeed, our gains will far outweigh our losses.

TIME

Rates of social change

Almost everyone yearns for some stability and predictability in his world, and therefore automatically resists some changes. According to Hoffer (1951), the recently poor and those poor who in some way sense what is possible most readily accept or cause change. The massive resistance to rapid social change shown by the corporate state is axiomatic (Reich, 1970). Whether or not one agrees entirely or in part with Hoffer or Reich, one conclusion is certain: If we do not change some of our ways quickly and drastically, we are certainly doomed. Some observers are concerned that doom may not come as quickly as predicted, thus resulting in decreased credibility for conservationists. There is little reason for this concern; first because the doom timetables may be correct, and second because our environmental predicament cannot be ignored, whether or not individuals are.

We have been and are sliding toward oblivion at a constantly accelerating rate (Meadows et al., 1972). This is why, on purely practical, hard-headed economic grounds as well as on social and aesthetic ones, it is extremely important to act quickly. Our ability to redirect our impact on the environment is limited. We may delay too long. Only when we have secured our safety should we be willing to sit back and listen to arguments that we could have waited a day, a year, or a decade longer.

What is ahead of us if we do act? There will surely be the satisfaction of feeling that we are accomplishing something really worthwhile. What has happened to others who have acted? What can we learn from them? In 1956, Rudd and Genelly published a book detailing what was then known about DDT, based on their own findings and on an intensive search of the literature. This had little or no immediate effect on the use of DDT, but it did educate some scientists, and it was one of these, Rachel Carson, who wrote *Silent Spring*. She used her skill as a writer to say in forceful language: Stop! You are surely doing harm with your pesticides and neither you nor anybody else can guess how deleterious your actions may be.

What did this brave woman receive for her successful turning of the pesticide tide? She received strong support, friendship, and admiration from some; vilification, ridicule, and hate from many others. Scientists, many of them directly or indirectly in the employ of the pesticide industry, wrote and spoke against her and her book.

Russian roulette

Few, if any, on either side showed that a difference in philosophy was at the root of the argument. Even the most money-mad industrialist will not knowingly sign his own death warrant. However, his desire for money and the power it brings may blind him to many realities. Conservationists have been saying, "Let's make sure things are safe before we use them." Those who fought Rachel Carson were saying, "Let's use them and then if we find they are deleterious, we can stop." Rachel Carson, with her understanding of ecology, could see how terribly dangerous the latter approach is. She saw that such an approach is like playing Russian roulette; before you learn that the live round is in the chamber under the pistol's hammer, you are dead. As Woodwell, Craig, and Johnson (1971) have said, "What is clear is that large quantities of DDT were introduced into use before any appraisal was made of the capacity of the biosphere for receiving them. In this instance man seems to have been blessed with extraordinary good fortune." DDT has caused great ecological mischief, but much less mischief than it might have caused based upon our meager ecological knowledge.

Those who have fought for continued use of persistent pesticides, for continued use of lead in gasoline, and so on, either unthinkingly or in ignorance have no fears of the ecological consequences. Or perhaps the potential monetary rewards lead them to put these worrisome possibilities out of their minds. They choose to ignore the fact that one of the revolver chambers surely has a bullet in it, because the rewards are so great for clicking the hammer on the empty chambers. The big difference of course is that in Russian roulette only the player dies.

The future?

What is in store for us if we are to survive? One can guess that we will probably see a leveling off of human population growth worldwide by about 1985, and the beginning of a significant population decline by 2000. These dates may seem to be a long way away. In terms of what must be accomplished in the interim, they are frighteningly near. We can expect to see the virtual elimination of the internal combustion engine or, if not, drastic reductions in its polluting ability. Similarly, we can expect a drastic per-capita decrease in power consumption in technologically advanced countries, with little per-capita increase in developing countries. This trend might be altered if safe and waste-free nuclear fusion techniques can be developed. It might also be altered if new and ecologically safe means of capturing and storing tide and wind energy are developed. More effective use of photosynthesis, and of mechanical and chemical means for harnessing solar energy, may become especially important in dealing with the energy crisis. Geothermal energy may also become very important. In our planning we dare not rely on such potential sources of energy. We will be playing Russian roulette again if we do.

We can probably also expect an increase in autocratic government, and an overall reduction in personal freedom both in amount and kind as population increases. In the U.S.A. our freedom-loving forefathers have already committed us to these conditions by their exuberant reproduction and their desire for personal gain through technology. This will continue a trend that has been under way for many years. Our much appreciated and much vaunted freedom is constantly being more and more circumscribed. How would Lincoln have reacted if he had been told to obtain a permit before he could build a front porch on his log cabin, as you and I must if we live in almost any American municipality. In fact, nowadays his cabin would probably be condemned and torn down.

In *The Greening of America* (1970), Reich sees developing in the U.S.A. a possible solution to the constant erosion of personal freedom. This solution may just possibly work, in spite of dense human populations. In essence, he points out that people can and are changing their life-styles to make their existence meaningful. With such changes occurring, changes in the social superstructure must follow. There is evidence that the process is under way. Instead of a man serving the corporate state as his master, he will serve himself and his fellow man equally, thereby forcing dissolution of the corporate state. According to Reich, man is turning from a termitelike existence to existence as a human. Instead of serving technology he is insisting that technology serve him. This is a very hopeful idea, especially because it has the potential to help everyone.

If in the years ahead we measure our standard of living in terms of material goods that people in "advanced" societies have and consume, those of us living in such societies will suffer a drastic decrease in our standard of living. Hopefully, this will be matched by a slight improvement in the material standards of developing countries. Unfortunately, the decrease in advanced countries may prove inadequate even to maintain the status quo in developing countries. The poor in industrialized countries will probably fare better, and may become the only group to experience gains in material wealth.

But standard of living is falsely measured in material wealth alone. We will all make some real gains. We can expect an eventual decrease in psychological disease—and psychologically caused diseases are just as real as those caused by biological pathogens. As a result, we will experience an eventual decrease in violence and war if we survive the dangerous years just ahead. Our foods will be safer, our air pure and clear, our waters more clear and potable, and our surroundings more pleasant to live in. We will regain the feeling that we can look with hope and pleasure toward the future of our children. Hopefully, we will eventually achieve the knowledge that mankind *is* on the way toward making things right with the world, and this will yield a degree of serenity that few experience these days. Utopian perhaps? Why not?

LEAVING OPTIONS

Excessive human population

Our survival on earth demands that we leave ourselves options in case we need them. Excessive population, probably more than any other factor except widespread radioactive contamination, reduces the possible choices for mankind. As population becomes excessive, either fewer and fewer can experience the benefits of advancing technology, or all must agree to live with fewer benefits than would be possible were the population smaller. Moreover, if human population outstrips the food supply necessary for everyone to have a subsistence diet, it would be social suicide to share the food equally, for all would starve. Under such circumstances there would be little reason to consider options that influence life's quality. The struggle for survival would only become a ferocious effort to control more resources than others do, forcing their death while ensuring one's own survival. No other alternative short of active or passive suicide seems possible. The leaving of options for the future is not a passive act. Our most urgent needs are to institute new ways of life in order to provide options for the future. One such obvious need is to depress quickly and adequately the worldwide birth rate as a humane way to stabilize world population. The alternative means to achieve population stabilization is to increase the death rate. Delay in reducing natality will ensure an increase in mortality. As Caldwell (1972) notes, ''. . . the crisis is concerned with the kind of creature that man is and with what he must become in order to survive. And what man can become must not only be individually motivated—it needs also to be socially assisted.''

Stabilization of human population must come *very* soon, because of the delays caused by the age structure. As Meadows et al. (1972) point out, if the replacement-size family were reached worldwide by the year 2000, the population would then be 5.8 billion and would rise to 8.2 billion before finally leveling off. (Billion as used in this book is 1000 million, the European milliard or 1.0×10^9.) In view of our present inadequately fed and strife-torn world population of 3.6 billion (in 1970), it appears certain, as a sociological estimate, that this will not happen. Well before the attainment of an 8.2 billion population, mortality will rise to stabilize or decrease the world population. Making no sociological estimates at all, the results from computer modeling led Meadows et al. (1972) to expect a large rise in the death rate before such a world population is achieved.

To summarize, it seems certain that the replacement-size family *will* be achieved worldwide before the year 2000. The more quickly and successfully humane means are employed, the less importance increased death rate will have in its achievement. The more delay there is in achieving the replacement-size family, the more savage will be the methods by which it is achieved, and the greater will be the chance that a sharp population decline will result. Some of that savagery is already apparent in the wars being waged around the world today. We do not have the 27 years from 1973 to 2000 to attain the replacement-size family by humane methods. It is not at all safe to assume that we have even 10 years. One cannot overestimate the urgency of this situation.

The expanding industrial production

Another example of an essential and difficult action needed to preserve alternatives is the stabilization of capital so that, on the average, investment capital matches depreciation. In a world accustomed to an expanding economy, this will be almost as difficult to achieve as it is essential. As Meadows et al. (1972) have shown, failure to stabilize capital will quickly negate any improvement achieved through stabilization of global human population. In their computer simulations of human destiny to the year 2100, it seems clear that resource depletion and/or pollution will cause greatly increased human mortality unless industrial activity, hence capital, is stabilized.

Much evidence indicates that control of a minor portion of industrial pollution would not be costly, but that complete pollution control would be very expensive and in many cases impossible. Thus some pollution will come from industry of any kind, and from many agricultural practices. Capital is increasing much faster than the exponentially increasing world human population. Much of this capital is used to expand industry. Thus even with a great effort directed toward pollution control, industry will quickly expand so that the actual amount of pollution produced will increase exponentially. Such an increase will quickly elevate the human death rate and the death rate of other organisms, causing collapse of the world ecosystem. Even assuming immediate and complete control of pollution, which is *an impossibility,* depletion of nonrenewable resources will cause the collapse of the industrial system. A rapid rise in the death rate would then be expected. Thus, if we are to conserve man, it is apparently as necessary that capital soon be no greater than depreciation as it is that births not exceed deaths. Since we must accomplish both goals, we can only assume they will be relatively humanely achieved if we consider the conservation aspects of man's existence. But it is hardly reassuring to read, "In short, large numbers of men are now redundant and for the survival of the species, are, unhappily, expendable" (Caldwell, 1972).

In order that we can be assisted in our search for a satisfying life, we may eventually need to determine for each personality type the optimum intercept of population density, amount and kind of technology, and the kind and distribution of natural, environmental, and aesthetic factors. Although this will not happen very soon, there is no reason to delay in directing studies toward this end. Investigations related to this problem have been under way for several years (McHarg, 1969).

We do not have enough of this type of information to help us much in planning our uses of the earth's resources. Since perhaps the very survival of life on earth and not just of man hinges on our actions relative to our environment, it is exceedingly important that we commit no irreparable environmental injustices.

Ecological knowledge and pesticides

It is in making evaluations of potential environmental damage that ecologists and nonecologists so often part company. For example, ecologists are aware of our inadequate knowledge concerning the effects of global distribution of persistent pesticides. The average person, lacking knowledge of the exceedingly intricate workings of the world's ecosystems, sees no reason to stop using something that provides him with such obvious benefits. "Besides," he thinks, "if there is any real problem the scientists will solve it for us."

Ecologists realize how little is known and how potentially great the damage caused by a pesticide may be. The average person, for example, can see no reason for not going ahead with use of a persistent chemical until it is positively shown that deleterious effects outweigh advantages. As a result we now have global pollution by DDT. Quite possibly the extermination of several vertebrate species will occur, even though the use of DDT is slowly being halted. We may lose some species even if the use of DDT is immediately halted worldwide. These are primarily species high on the food pyramid, which receive biologically concentrated doses of persistent pesticides (Fig. 2–2). Examples are the peregrine falcon *(Falco peregrinus)* and the brown pelican *(Pelecanus occidentalis)* (Anonymous, 1972; Blus et al., 1971; Enderson and Berger, 1970; Harte and Socolow, 1971; Hickey, 1969; and Woodwell, Craig, and Johnson, 1971).

The peregrine in its tremendous stoops (dives) is perhaps the fastest flying bird of prey in the world, and is the bird most generally favored by the falconer. It has been held in esteem for several centuries in Europe. Falconry was probably introduced into Britain in about A.D. 860. Falconry, probably involving peregrines, dates back to 2000 B.C. in China (Encyclopedia Brittanica, 1946).

The insects against which DDT is aimed will probably survive it very well. The fact that many insects, including malaria mosquitoes in many areas, are immune to its direct effects is not at all surprising (Anonymous, 1972). It is possible to breed fruit flies *(Drosophila melanogaster)* that are unaffected by DDT by selecting them for genetic resistance to the insecticide. This type of resistance has now developed among many wild populations of insects. Unfortunately, birds have little chance of becoming genetically resistant. They reproduce at a much slower rate and, most important, DDT prevents their successful reproduction.

What of the other persistent pesticides? And especially what of the hordes of new chemicals constantly being released into our environment? What will be their long-term effects? How many of our resource options have they already consumed?

Before any chemical agent proposed for general and widespread usage is released, its biodegradability should be determined. "It is possible to predetermine biodegradability of organic compounds—the technology has long existed," according to Payne, Wiebe, and Christian (1970), who also comment that biodegradation will not occur at an acceptable rate in ". . . aldrin, dieldrin, endrin, toxiphene, heptachlor, DDT or DDE, benzene hexachloride, chlordane, and others." Some recalcitrants (chemicals that are not readily biodegradable) actually damage the microorganisms we depend upon for biodegradation. For example, in one detergent there are isomers that inhibit bacteria that would otherwise degrade some of its other isomers. "If these hazardous compounds are sufficiently . . . effective in the task for which they were . . . designed, research directed toward synthesis of similar but degradable isomers or substitutes should clearly be continued. But meanwhile, expediency notwithstanding, reason demands that use of nondegradable substances should be strictly limited in order to obviate the danger of long term damage in nature" (Payne, Wiebe, and Christian, 1970). Their use should be limited solely to laboratory testing, except in extreme cases in which the decision to use them elsewhere should be made by someone other than the person who would profit from the use.

Radioactive contamination

In the August 23, 1970, issue of *The Times-Standard* of Eureka, California, is an Associated Press dispatch (page 21) reporting the results of certain nuclear weapon tests in 1958. To verify that the crash of a U.S. bomber would not trigger a nuclear explosion, a crash was simulated at the Atomic Energy Commission (AEC) Nevada test site. A bomb's high-explosive charge was detonated without first electronically arming the nuclear warhead. As was expected, this failed to produce a nuclear explosion, but it scattered plutonium over a 250-square-mile area (647.5 square kilometers). If one accepts that nuclear bombs will be carried around in aircraft in "peacetime," this test was probably necessary. Perhaps, though, it need not have been made above ground. Since then at least two actual crashes have occurred.

Within the plutonium-contaminated areas that resulted from the simulated crash are 49 "hot" areas fenced off because they are too radioactive to permit human access. In total these areas encompass 12 square miles (31 square kilometers). Remembering that ". . . one milligram of plutonium is a lethal dose to the average human being" (White, 1948), one can see that this does not mean that there is necessarily very much of the material in these areas. However, it does mean that there is still some plutonium contamination over a very large area. White (1948) refers to direct lethality. As a carcinogen, plutonium is much more dangerous (Gofman and Tamplin, 1971). According to the AEC, the amount of plutonium picked up and scattered by the wind in this desert area is not hazardous, however, such statements are now being very seriously challenged [Gofman and Tamplin (1971); also Gillette (1972) for other similar challenges of AEC safety efforts]. The half-life of this plutonium isotope is 24,360 years. If the badly contaminated 12 square miles are ever to be reoccupied by man, it will probably not be for at least three times that many years.

What are the options for those that follow us? These plutonium-contaminated areas, barring special clean-up operations, are, as far as the support of man is concerned, essentially useless—almost as if we had cut a 12-square-mile chunk out of the earth and thrown it away into space. What of the wildlife that may visit these areas? What of the biological concentration of the radioactivity they carry away with them? What does this mean in terms of the amount of radioactivity released from applications of nuclear energy in medicine and for public power? These are the kinds of important questions that are too infrequently asked. Man's survival, not just his health and happiness, rests on preserving options.

SUGGESTED DISCUSSION MATERIAL

1. Investigate Native American culture and find examples of social mores that result in conservation of resources. How and why might these have come into existence? Do archeological and paleontological records give any clues?

2. Explore case histories of international aid and of aid given within your own country. What have been the social and conservational results?

3. How do you and your classmates feel about the ability of science and technology to solve the major conservation problems facing the world? Try returning to this question after you have finished the course. Have any of you changed your minds? If so, in what way?

4. Investigate the means by which population stabilization can be achieved. Discuss the feelings of minorities in their struggles for power and how these relate to population control. How do these feelings relate to the political struggles between nations? Is there any way these negative feelings can be utilized to achieve stabilization of population by humane means?

5. Explore the literature of the AEC and also that of its critics. Set up a discussion allowing full cross-examination of witnesses. Explore in depth the uses of atomic energy and its possible implications for mankind.

6. Some revolutionaries speak of underpopulation even in countries where starvation is already commonplace. What reason(s) do they have for this? Find out what you can about past and present population policies in various countries, and relate your findings to world politics, social mores, and religious and parareligious motivation.

Peters

Ecology

2

A brief review of ecological principles of specific significance for conservation will set the stage for the rest of this book. This chapter emphasizes the ecological factors that most frequently seem to be important in conservation decision making.

Ecology forms the foundation of conservation, together with human-oriented disciplines such as anthropology, psychology, economics, sociology, political science, and human ecology. Ecology in turn is based on botany, zoology, meteorology, physics, chemistry, mathematics, soil science, geology, and so on. All disciplines, including the arts and humanities, are related to ecology because ecology by definition is the study (*logos,* Greek) of the home (*oikos,* Greek) and is interpreted broadly as the study of the interrelations of organisms and their environments.

Such studies can be approached from an almost infinite number of directions. For instance, one can logically study environmental perception in order to identify and quantify human standards of aesthetic "goodness" and "badness" (Lowenthal, 1968). One can also study mathematical models to optimize strategy for uses of resources (Watt, 1968). Indeed, the first type of study can provide important data for the mathematical studies. Both are in a sense ecological studies, although certainly not of the traditional kind, and both yield exciting and practical insights for the solution of conservation problems.

FINITENESS AND INTERRELATEDNESS OF RESOURCES

We hear of the limitless wealth of the sea, but actually it is far from limitless (Anonymous, 1972). Perhaps the only resources we have that could possibly be considered infinite are energy from the sun and energy from atomic nuclei. Technological advances will be necessary if we are to tap the vast energy of nuclear fusion (Weinberg, 1971).

Energy pathways

It is important to understand the interrelatedness of things. These interrelations are well illustrated when we explore the pathways solar energy may follow in passing through an ecosystem (Fig. 2–1). After its capture and utilization by a green plant, this energy may pass through a *herbivore,* a *carnivore,* and *decomposers,* and finally be reradiated to space. At every step heat is produced. Although heat is useful to organisms in colder environments, it is not usable by them as an energy source for processes such as movement or growth. Thus heat energy is lost at every step, and we find in organisms special mechanisms for carrying out chemical reactions with the production of minimum amounts of heat, and also mechanisms for disposing of excess heat. The complex enzyme-mediated metabolism of plants and animals are examples of heat control in biotic chemical reactions. The flapping ears of the African elephant (*Loxodonta africana*), the countercurrent heat-exchanging circulatory system in the flukes of great whales, the orientation of leaves edge-on to the sun in

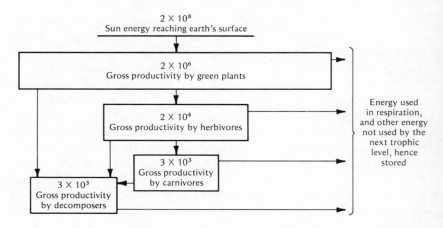

Figure 2–1. Energy Relationships. The figures are rough approximations and are given in gram calories per square meter per year. The arrows indicate movement or flow of energy. The lengths of the arrows indicating stored energy and energy of respiration are roughly proportional to the relative amounts (percent) of energy from each trophic level that take this pathway. (Compiled from various sources.)

compass plants, and leaf cooling through evaporation of water are examples of biotic mechanisms helping organisms to control heat.

Food pathways

If Fig. 2–1 is inverted, an exploded view of the usual biotic or food pyramid can be seen. By assigning names of single living things to the appropriate blocks in sequence, a food chain can be constructed. In very simple terms this might be: a grass—a cow—a man—a decomposer species. In south central Africa it might be: a mopane *(Collophosporum mopane)*[1] tree—an elephant—a man—a decomposer species. By tracing many of the possible pathways to each *trophic level* (*trophikos,* Greek: feeding) shown by the labeled blocks, you may diagram any number of *food webs.* For example, the mopane tree is fed upon by a large caterpillar which is much sought after for human food; the mopane foliage and smaller branches are also fed upon by impala *(Aepyceros melampus),* eland *(Taurotragus oryx),* kudu *(Tragelaphus strepsiceros),* elephant, and so on.

Each of the herbivores that feeds on it may in turn be eaten by any of several *carnivores* or *insectivores;* furthermore, carnivores may feed on other carnivores or feed on *omnivores* as illustrated by lions *(Panthera leo)* eating humans. Each animal, as well as its droppings and urine, may be in part decomposed by a great many species of decomposers from bacteria to flies and dung beetles, and perhaps we should even include vultures (Family Cathartidae), bateleur eagles *(Terathopius ecaudatus),* hyenas *(Crocuta crocuta* and *Hyaena brunnea),* jackals (*Canis* spp.), and, yes, man.

Man is a part of every trophic level above green plants. Businessmen call us consumers, and we are. Ecologists call green plants *producers,* and here business terminology no longer fits. *Consumer* animals, such as ourselves, that feed on both plants and animals are termed *omnivores.* Actually, very few mammals are exclusively herbivorous or carnivorous. Many ants and grasshoppers have been munched down by bison, and many pieces of plant material have at least contaminated the meat swallowed by lions. In fact, an internal parasite of herbivores, *Dicrocoelium dendriticum,* utilizes ants as intermediate hosts. Eggs from adult worms in sheep, deer, rabbits, or sometimes even man pass out in the host's feces. The eggs are eaten by land snails and develop inside them. The resulting cercariae are deposited in small slime balls by the snails, and ants that eat the slime balls acquire the cercariae. When an ant is accidentally eaten by a herbivore or by man, the cercariae develop into adult reproductive

[1]Pronounced mó-pah-nee.

parasites, and the cycle is complete (Davis and Anderson, 1971; Krull, 1969).

ECOSYSTEMS AND BIOTIC COMMUNITIES

Any carnivorous, piscivorous, or insectivorous animal swallowing small prey whole consumes the vegetation-laden stomach and intestinal contents, as we do when we eat clams, oysters, and sardines. This vegetative material and also the body of the prey are composed of chemical elements required by living organisms. All organisms acquire these elements from their environment; for example, the aardwolf *(Proteles cristatus)* obtains them from the termites it eats, and floating duckweed (*Lemna* spp.), a favorite food of ducks, obtains its chemicals from the water in which it floats. In a closed ecosystem these elements cycle or circulate between the living and the nonliving parts of the system. This helps us to characterize an ecosystem. Energy flows through ecosystems, while chemical elements cycle between the *biotic* (living) and the *abiotic* (nonliving) parts within them.

To show the cycling of elements, it is common to discuss the *carbon cycle* or the *hydrologic* (water) *cycle,* showing the fixation of atmospheric carbon by green plants and its eventual return to the atmosphere, or the movement of water to the clouds through organisms, through soil, and so on. Likewise, other materials cycle. Figure 2–2 shows the movement of DDT and its sequel DDE within an ecosystem which includes a temperate-zone lake. This is an incomplete cycle because some of its parts are unknown, and because DDE is eventually degraded chemically.

Biotic community and ecological niche

In the cycle the insecticide (DDT or DDE) moves back and forth between the living and the nonliving parts of the ecosystem. The living part is composed of one or more *biotic communities.* A biotic community is a more-or-less integrated association of interacting living organisms. Each species within the biotic community occupies a unique physical position and role, its *ecological niche.* This niche is determined not only by abiotic factors of the environment such as climate, but also by biotic factors such as the other plants and animals present. To illustrate the importance of biotic factors in determining an ecological niche, we consider the introduction of snowshoe hares *(Lepus americanus)* into Newfoundland.

Prior to 1864 (Dodds, 1965), Newfoundland was populated with Arctic hares *(Lepus arcticus)* but lacked snowshoe hares. Arctic hares occurred on mountaintops and also in the extensive spruce forests be-

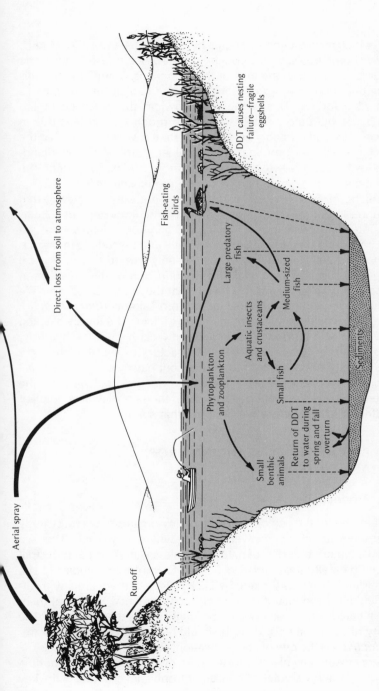

Figure 2–2. DDT–DDE cycle in an aquatic ecosystem. Each time an organism is eaten, its insecticide burden is stored by the consumer. Thus piscivorous birds such as loons (*Gavia* spp.) and grebes (family Podicipedidae), large predatory fish such as bass (*Micropterus* spp.) and pike (*Esox lucius*), and also man receive biologically concentrated DDT or DDE. In a temperate-zone lake, the insecticide that reaches the sediments is redispersed into the water twice yearly, during spring and fall overturns. Since DDE is slowly broken down, this cycle is different from the cycle of an element such as carbon in that it will slowly run down after the input of DDT by man stops. (Compiled from various sources.)

Aerial spray

Direct loss from soil to atmosphere

Runoff

Fish-eating birds

DDT causes nesting failure—fragile eggshells

Large predatory fish

Medium-sized fish

Aquatic insects and crustaceans

Small fish

Phytoplankton and zooplankton

Small benthic animals

Return of DDT to water during spring and fall overturn

Sediments

tween. After their introduction sometime between 1864 and 1876 (Dodds, 1965), snowshoe hares spread throughout the spruce forests, and Arctic hares became restricted to the tops of the mountains. Some interpret this as meaning that mountaintops constitute a better habitat for Arctic hares than do spruce forests. This is the case now, in the presence of the snowshoe hares, but unfortunately there is no proof that this was true in their absence. We will probably never know, for it is very unlikely that the snowshoe hare will ever be completely eliminated from Newfoundland. All we can say is that in Newfoundland *with snowshoe hares present,* the ecological niche of the Arctic hare is on the mountaintops.

The niche of an animal or plant includes not only everything that impinges upon it, but also the times at which these impingements occur. Since the potential interactions are infinite in number, it follows that we can never be certain that any organism can live and reproduce in a situation it is not presently occupying. Thus the only true test of ecological suitability is the successful survival and reproduction of the organism in that situation. In practical terms this means that the only method we have to determine, for example, whether or not red salmon *(Oncorhynchus nerka)* can successfully spawn and their eggs hatch in a previously blocked stream in Alaska is to introduce some and see what happens. Obviously, we should measure certain environmental factors to see that they are within the range of tolerance for red salmon; but having done this we still will not know the chance of survival and reproduction until we plant the salmon there and observe what happens. Even then we may have to plant several different strains before we find one that survives.

PRODUCTIVITY, STANDING CROP, AND NUTRITION

Productivity

To understand better the ecological niche of any organism, we must study areas where they are absent, as well as those where they occur. Thus we need to make intensive studies of naturally fishless waters and of terrestrial areas having naturally impoverished faunas. Examples are studies of the Galapagos Islands, such as the one by Lack (1947). If there are any trout-free lakes left in the mountains of western North America, studies of them should be initiated before someone unthinkingly stocks them with fish. The productivity of such waters and lands should be one of the factors examined. *Productivity* is the rate of energy fixation. *Primary productivity* is the **rate** of energy fixation by plants, mostly green ones. *Secondary productivity* is the rate of energy storage at consumer trophic levels. **Rate** is the key word.

Sometimes it is useful to talk about *gross* and *net* primary productivity. The gross primary productivity of a paper birch tree *(Betula papyrifera)* is the total photosynthesis of that tree over a specified time span, for example, from the time the leaves flush in the spring until they drop in the fall. The net primary productivity of the tree is what is left in total tree growth at the end of the growing year, including leaves removed by insects, buds removed by grouse, rootlets that died and decayed, and so on. Much of the sugar produced in photosynthesis is utilized within a plant for its own metabolic processes and therefore does not show up in tree growth. Most such energy eventually leaves the plant as heat.

Since no process carried on by consumers is comparable to photosynthesis, it is best not to speak of gross and net secondary productivity. However, this usage occurs in the literature and refers to subdivisions most nearly comparable to parts of net primary productivity in green plants.

The term productivity is also used by agriculturalists who often confront us with data on agricultural productivity. The productivity of maize is usually measured in bushels or sacks per acre or hectare. This is only remotely related to and is much less than the net primary productivity measured by ecologists.

Standing crop

One of the reasons why many people do not understand that removing females of a wildlife meat species maximizes the production of meat is that they do not distinguish between *productivity* and *standing crop*. Productivity is a rate, whereas standing crop is simply a measure of what is present at any particular instant. We measure standing crop in terms such as deer per square mile, or board feet of timber per acre. This often has little relationship to the rate of production of deer meat or wood. Stunted deer populations, as well as stunted fish populations, are well known. Somehow it is easier for people to accept that fish populations must be reduced if one is to obtain good individual growth than to accept that the same is true of deer.

Effects of malnourishment

Figure 2–3 shows "Scudder" with his first set of antlers. He is an orphaned black-tailed deer *(Odocoileus hemionus)* a little over 1 year old and was raised on a bottle. Wild deer of Scudder's home area have little, 3-inch-long spikes at his age. The much larger antlers that Scudder "wears" result from the excellent feeding he has had. Scudder is also considerably larger than his wild brothers. He illustrates why productivity of meat may actually go up when standing crop goes down, and feeding conditions improve as

Figure 2–3. Black-tailed deer, *Odocoileus hemionus,* reared at California State University, Humboldt. When this photograph was taken, he was about 1.5 years old, and these were his first antlers. Had he not damaged them on the fence, they would have been even larger. Wild yearlings in the area from which he was obtained have at best 3-inch-long spike antlers. Good feeding has made the difference.

a consequence. He is a legal buck in California, while the wild males of his age are not. This is part of the reason why either-sex deer hunting is frequently accompanied by an increasing kill of bucks.

Food sources are the ultimate determiners of biomass. Thus the productivity at any level has a direct bearing on the other levels above it in the biotic pyramid. The stunting of malnourished individuals is not limited to fish and deer. It happens in almost all living things, including humans.

In humans the evidence is becoming very strong that inadequate nutrition *in utero* and during early childhood leads to permanent mental impairment as well as physical stunting. There is every reason to think that, if that is true of humans, it must also be true of other animals. This may be yet another mechanism that helps to assure intraspecific control of population size and/or its ecological effects. Natural selection probably favors populations that avoid starvation and any resulting decrease in mental ability, for their long-term existence is thereby better assured.

Intelligence assists mammals in their survival under natural conditions. We may find that nutritionally deprived prey animals are especially vulnerable to predation, not only because they are physically smaller and weaker, but also because they are mentally inferior. Just as such nutritional deprivation has an effect on prey, it probably also affects predators. In general, predators seem to have greater behavioral plasticity than their prey. If so, insufficient nutrition may have its greatest impact on predators. Should these possible nutritional effects on the intelligence of predators and prey hold true, upon a decrease in prey numbers, exceptionally rapid declines in predation should occur after a time lag.

In the future we could perhaps construct hypothetical models describing the population effects of nutritional deprivation on wolves and deer. In the southern parts of the wolf *(Canis lupus)* range in North America, deer are the most important prey. To make our models realistic we must take into account the effects of parasites shared by the two, other causes of mortality and debility in deer, and alternate prey for the wolves. We also must consider parasites, and the causes of death and debility in these alternate prey, as well as factors that affect birthrate, infant survival, and intelligence. The complexity of these interrelationships results from biotic diversity which in itself is worth studying. We return to a consideration of biotic diversity after laying a little more groundwork.

PHYSICAL AND BIOLOGICAL ORGANIZATION

We are aware of organization at the subatomic level. We know physicists can build atomic bombs which terrorize us. Because they are not exploding at random, we have confidence in physical order and predictability at the subatomic and molecular levels. We are also aware that celestial events are predictable, because the sun rises in the east when we predict it will, the moon waxes and wanes on schedule, and the North Star or Southern Cross stays in the same place relative to our neighbor's chimney.

Between these examples of micro- and macroorganization are other familiar levels. Individual organisms are beautifully integrated whether viruses, bacteria, algae, redwoods, ants, or whales. Within species we see organization in colonies of social insects and in host—parasite relationships, to say nothing of human societies. We also see organization that allows prediction at still higher levels, for example, evolution and ecological succession are such ordered processes.

Recognition of organization allows predictions to be made at levels from the subatomic to the celestial. One wonders why we seem to be less accurate in our predictions of ecological phenomena than we are in almost any other realm of scientific endeavor. It almost appears as if the great complexity of celestial phenomena causes an "averaging out" which has simplified the gross predictions made thus far in man's history. Perhaps ecology is so much a part of us, and we of it, that we "cannot see the forest for the trees." Ecology is also an extremely complex field, and because we are so close to it we find its complexity nearly impossible to ignore. Probably, many of the necessary advances in ecological understanding will come only after large-scale, interdisciplinary research efforts. What are some of the more predictable events in ecology? Biotic succession is one.

BIOTIC SUCCESSION

Given enough time, a large, bare rock outcrop will be colonized by plants (Figs. 2–4 and 2–5). As time passes, the original algae will be sequentially replaced by lichens, mosses, grasses, forbs, shrubs, and finally trees—if the outcrop is situated in an area moist enough to support tree growth. As this succession of plant communities with its associated animals progresses, the climatic conditions immediately adjacent to the rock become more

Figure 2–4. Primary biotic succession on a rock outcrop called a "kopje" in southern Africa. This is a dry site in a dry climatic region. Contrast with Fig. 2–5, taken in an area with more rainfall.

Figure 2–5. Primary biotic succession on a rock outcrop in Malawi. A rainstorm had just passed. Note that the flat top of the rock supports forest vegetation. This releases water to the steeper face, making it more mesic, hence speeding succession on it. The steepness alone is probably responsible for the lack of seed plants on the face. Contrast with Fig. 2–4.

and more *mesic* (moderately moist). That is, microclimatic conditions come to approximate the middle of the possible climatic range between dry and wet at that geographic location.

Successions that start with bare rock are termed *primary successions;* so also are those that start with open water in a rock basin. If a succession starts on soil that has had some or all of its living organisms removed, it is called a *secondary succession.* Succession starting on bare rock constantly bathed by spray from a waterfall is quite different from that at a dry site.

Moving away from a pond one often observes a series of communi-

Figure 2–6. Hydric succession in a coastal dune pond and marsh near Arcata, California. Note the submerged and emergent aquatic plants in the foreground, and the emergent vegetation and willows on the opposite shore. Across the marsh in the distance lie pine-covered dunes. As the dunes rise beyond the marsh, the sites become progressively drier. This gives rise to a vegetative ecocline.

ties (Fig. 2–6). The first changes are successional, but as one travels toward higher ground, site factors such as soil moisture become more and more limiting. Such a series of more-or-less intergrading communities is termed an *ecocline*. Many occurrences can disrupt the orderly succession of biotic communities before the establishment of a final, self-replacing, biotic community, a *climax* community. These same factors may also disturb a climax community, again initiating successional changes. One of the most common of these is fire. Fire is so prevalent in some places that it tends to maintain for long periods biotic communities especially adapted to its presence. These have been called fire *disclimaxes*. The chaparral of coastal California and the comparable brushlands of the Mediterranean shores and the coast of South Africa are examples (Fig. 2–7). We discuss fire in more detail later (page 78).

Feeding and trampling by herbivorous mammals are also important both in setting back succession and in maintaining communities by altering or delaying succession (Figs. 4–1 and 4–2). Their activities often interact with fire, affecting a community in important ways (see page 83).

Chance factors

Climax communities, by definition, reproduce themselves in the same location, whereas in the absence of disturbances such as fire or grazing successional communities do not. Both chance and the diverse capabilities of organisms play a role in determining the details of biotic succession.

The role of what we call chance is illustrated when we realize that the vegetation following a fire is partly determined by what seeds are present in the soil. Even on the same site, the relative abundances of seeds from different species change from time to time. In addition, seed tolerance to heat differs among species, and the heat of the fire may also differ from one time or location to another.

Species capabilities

Species differences in heat tolerance illustrate the variation in capabilities of organisms. Another example is the ability of plants to carry on photosynthesis at low temperatures. Some conifers are capable of photosynthesis at −35°C, while most tropical species cannot photosynthesize at temperatures below +5°C (Meyer and Anderson, 1939, pp. 354–355). While this example presents the extremes, within any biota there is a lesser but ecologically important range of tolerance to environmental factors. These differences have much to do with the actual biotic makeup of the community.

The factors involved in organism capability are more complex than one might at first expect. For example, an organism may tolerate temperatures between −40°C and +50°C but grow and reproduce best at +25 °C. However, its optimum temperature for withstanding desiccating conditions may be about −15°C in a natural environment. Such relationships may well determine the species present in a *seral* biotic community. Clearly, ecological factors are interrelated; a change in one affects many, if not all. Furthermore, many organisms do better under the fluctuating conditions of nature than they do under constant conditions.

Organisms are not merely passive recipients of whatever the environment offers. They alter their own environments and those of other organisms. Mobile organisms actively seek optimum environments for meeting their own changing requirements.

Figure 2–7. Experimental fire in chaparral on the Hopland Research Station of the University of California. Many chaparral plants sprout profusely from the root crown after being burned. Black-tailed deer avidly seek to browse this nutritious new growth. Fire is a common factor in chaparral areas.

COMPETITION

Some plants release antibiotic chemicals into the air and/or soils, effectively preventing other plants from living nearby. Some even thus poison themselves. (Man seems to be doing almost the same thing.) Some plants can survive in drier soil better than others can, and so may deplete soil water to a point where they cause the death of other plant species. Thus among plants, as among animals, there is competition for resources, the winner eliminating the loser. In recent literature this has been termed *competitive exclusion.*

The competition enigma

The more similar two organisms, the more intense and frequent their competition for resources in short supply when they live *sympatrically* (in the same area). Therefore competition between members of the same species *(intraspecific competition)* should be more intense than between members of different species *(interspecific competition);* yet how is this possible if competitive exclusion exists? The evidence from natural biotic communities indicates three ways in which this enigmatic situation is altered by natural selection: selection has favored intraspecific cooperative behavior, has modified intraspecific aggressive behavior so that it favors species welfare, and has resulted in the formation of new species. The coordination between members of a wolf pack during a hunt is an example of cooperation. Territoriality, which spaces breeding pairs of song sparrows thereby guaranteeing sufficient resources for raising nestlings, is an example of aggression that favors species welfare. Speciation through natural selection may occur with appropriate mixtures of *subspecific allopatry* (living in different areas) and sympatry. To explore examples of the effects of these factors in speciation, see Dobzhansky (1941), Sibley (1950), G. L. Stebbins (1949), and R. C. Stebbins (1950).

There is a similarity between the ability of a climax temperate deciduous forest community to reproduce itself and the cooperative utilization by many ants and termites of resources and their physiologically ensured dispersal in times of overpopulation. Each is the present end product of biological evolution through natural selection, a positive response to the advantages gained through a partial reduction in competition. Wouldn't it be nice if humans through their intelligence could do as well? It is our similarity to each other that guarantees the great advantages to be obtained through cooperation rather than competition. The ferocity seen in business and politics of the post-Darwinian era was rationalized as being natural. That was a misinterpretation of natural selection, for it is a reduction in direct competition that natural selection tends to achieve.[1] The evolutionary result of aggressive behavior is removal of damaging conflict. (Lorenz, 1966, Chapt. 14, pp. 275–299).

BIOTIC DIVERSITY

Reduction in competition through natural selection has led to speciation. Speciation and the movements of species across the earth have led to

[1]This is not to imply that any directive force controls genetic mutation. Reduction in competition results from the impact of natural selection upon genetically diverse populations of organisms.

increased species diversity. Many biotic communities have become rich in species whose interactions impart a balance-of-powers effect, increasing community stability (Anonymous, 1972). This result of biotic diversity is an important consideration when evaluating potential environmental manipulations.

The severity of the physical environment determines in part the possible options for viable genetic combinations. Thus arctic communities tend to lack diversity. For example, to inhabit a wintertime arctic environment requires special adaptations of homeothermic animals. Efficient insulation, some means of avoiding the general climate, large mass-to-surface ratio, special physiological or behavioral adaptations, or some combination of these is necessary for survival. Many arctic birds and mammals are large relative to their closely related more southern relatives (Bergmann's rule) and have shorter appendages (Allen's rule). Also, their fur or feathers usually insulate better than those of more southern forms. Another way some animals solve the problem is to live a *subnival* (below the snow) or *subterranean* (below the ground) life, thus avoiding the extremes of temperature found at the snow surface.

A mammal the size and shape of a least weasel *(Mustela rixosa)*, for example, could not live a weasel's life chasing rodents through their burrows, and carry around the fur insulation it would need, if it did not spend much of its time in winter below the snow. Snow forms an insulating layer which makes possible the survival of small species of mammals in the arctic. The ruffed grouse *(Bonasa umbellus)* of the timbered valleys also utilize this insulation, flying down into the snow to roost below its surface.

The cold and the short winter day or continuous night at higher latitudes combine to restrict severely the possibilities for diversity of organisms, plants as well as animals. In the tropics, on the contrary, climatic conditions leave great scope for biotic diversification. Here the long neck and long legs of giraffe *(Giraffa camelopardalis)* allow them to feed high and give no trouble with temperature control, in fact they may even help get rid of excess heat (Fig. 2–8). African wild dogs *(Lycaon pictus)* sport huge, erect, batlike ears excellent for scooping in the faintest sounds, but such ears would freeze off an arctic canid within a few hours in winter. The elegantly elongated gerenuk *(Lithocranius walleri)* can stand on its hind legs and stretch its long slender neck to browse in the lower branches of acacias *(Acacia* spp.) in East Africa. In the arctic such an animal would freeze to death, and no tall plants as the acacia trees could survive wind-driven granular snow blasting them for days on end.

It is also thought that part of the reason why the tropics show much greater biotic richness than arctic areas is that they were spared the great Pleistocene climatic changes that so strongly influenced the arctic and northern temperate areas. Instead of glaciation, they had *pluvial* (rainy)

Figure 2–8. Giraffes, *Giraffa camelopardalis,* at a pan in Wankie National Park, Rhodesia. Giraffes are perhaps the most highly specialized of browsing mammals. A tropical environment is probably essential for warm-blooded mammals with such elongated extremities. By carrying soil away from these pans on their bodies and in the water they drink, giraffes and other animals help to form and maintain these ponds.

periods. This allowed more time for the evolution of specialized forms in the tropics. Both the severity of the arctic environment and the long duration in the tropics of mild climactic conditions have probably helped to determine the striking differences in diversity between these two biotas today. Careful study of the biotas in geologically old tropical deserts, such as the Kalahari, could help us evaluate the relative importance of environmental severity and climatic stability as factors affecting biotic richness.

STABILITY, DIVERSITY, AND PRODUCTIVITY

Stability of biotic communities is related to their diversity and to their position in biotic succession. Climax communities reproduce themselves; hence in one sense they are more stable than successional communities.

Problems of community ordination

The long grass prairie–deciduous forest *ecotone* of North America serves as a useful example. Fire disclimaxes, which the long grass prairie is often considered to be, maintain themselves for very long periods. Frequent burning is necessary for their continued existence. When fires were halted by immigrant settlers, the long grass prairie progressed through successional stages toward a climax deciduous forest. In the presence of fire, and in this region, the prairie is the more stable community. Calling the prairie a disclimax implicitly assumes that the fires were unnatural. Humans probably set most of the fires, and probably had been doing so over the last 10,000–24,000 or perhaps even 50,000 years. Man with his fires was part of the ecosystem, and the time periods involved were sufficient to encompass major geological changes. On this basis one might consider the long grass prairie of North America a valid climax community, and fire a natural factor. In this instance the notion that climax communities are relatively stable can be supported.

It is not certain that successional communities are always less stable than the climax communities toward which they tend. Part of the reason is illustrated in the long grass prairie–deciduous forest situation discussed above. In this example disagreement over the definition of climax is expected. If the prairie is considered a successional stage between bare ground and climax temperate deciduous forest, the interpretation becomes exactly the opposite. The successional stage is the more stable, at least when subjected to fire. In a successional series it is often difficult to know exactly where a particular biotic community lies in the series relative to another similar community. When we attempt to compare such dissimilar entities as terrestrial arctic communities with tropical marine communities, the difficulties become great. The problems of community ordination alone make difficult the analysis of relative stability.

Problems in determining diversity and community boundaries

Analysis of biotic diversity is just as puzzling. In taking a detailed view, it is difficult to find valid and generally acceptable criteria by which to measure species diversity. Simple numbers of species and individuals fail miserably when one contemplates the relative impact of one mouse versus one elephant.

Another problem is to devise a generally acceptable and objective means to define the limits of biotic communities. With few if any exceptions, in any large region the greatest wealth of species and numbers results from the interspersion of a large number of communities at different successional stages (Leopold, 1933). It is not valid to compare a large area of one climax community with a comparable area possessing a great interspersion of successional types of communities and conclude that successional communities, meaning the whole area, are more diverse than climax ones. Yet, what criteria does one use to define the cut off point between what might be called macro- and microinterspersion? The most uniform natural community imaginable is not completely homogeneous. The answer to this question can strongly influence the outcome of any diversity estimate.

The global view

Another way to approach the analysis of biotic diversity is to take a very broad geographic view. We know that the number of species in the continental tropics is much higher than in temperate continental areas, and that the high Arctic and Antarctic continental areas have very few. There is evidence that the total biomass, metabolism, and productivity of these continental areas show the same trends. From this we might reasonably conclude that continental tropical communities on the average, or at least in the aggregate, are more diverse than comparable high Arctic and Antarctic communities. If this is so, we would expect communities of the continental tropics, at least in the aggregate, to be more stable than those of the high Arctic and Antarctic continental regions. In general they seem to be more stable.

Going from the tropics through the temperate to the Arctic regions, we find decreases in standing crops and in productivity of plants and animals. The small standing crops of arctic vegetation may not be so much the result of coldness per se as of the resulting inability of organisms to utilize water. Because of the cold soil, even in the summer, plant roots have difficulty obtaining water. In a sense, plants of the wet tundra live in a cold, wet desert. The standing crops of *plankton* (organisms that are propelled mostly by water currents) in Arctic and Antarctic oceans are often very large, and have high productivity (El-Sayed, 1967). As explained earlier, it is productivity that counts. One must remember that Arctic ocean water temperatures never drop much below about $-1.7°C$ (Fairbridge, 1966). This is a far cry from terrestrial surface temperatures which drop as low as $-68°C$. On the average, the highest biotic productivities are probably found in the tropics and the lowest at high latitudes, assuming equal availability of nutrients. The year-long growing season for terrestrial vegetation in the humid tropics ensures this.

POPULATION CONTROL

There is a theoretical upper limit to the size that population can reach. Actual populations seldom or never reach this limit. Productivity per reproductive unit is usually high at lower population levels, and becomes low when the peak is reached. Population limitation may be achieved by reduction in new individuals produced, reduction in the rate of growth, and/or loss of the individuals produced. Populations of organisms at low densities relative to the ability of the environment to support them tend to grow exponentially, that is, in a 2–4–8–16 . . . manner. Rapidly expanding populations often overshoot their environment's *carrying capacity* (its long-term ability to support them). At such times herbivores may feed on stored plant materials such as root reserves and stem growth of previous years.

Extrinsic and intrinsic mechanisms

Chapman (1928) used the term *environmental resistance* to describe the summation of all factors working on a population to restrict its increase. We now consider, as environmental resistance, only the extrinsic factors that help to control populations. In some species, internal physiological changes take place which also serve to control populations. These changes may work directly, or they may cause behavioral changes which reduce the population and/or cause animals to disperse. Virtually all animal species probably have one or more intrinsic mechanisms which halt their population growth if extrinsic factors such as disease or predation fail to do so (Wynne-Edwards, 1964). At the moment, however, this notion that *all* have intrinsic mechanisms to control their populations is hypothetical.

Intrinsic mechanisms are needed, because without them species are dependent on other species or physical factors of the environment to control their abundance. In a predator–prey situation, this requires that predators take prey just often enough to keep prey populations down, but never in numbers great enough to eliminate a prey species over any considerable area. It also requires that prey populations evolve escape mechanisms just adequate to balance the skills of the predators. A mutation in either population resulting in a considerable increase in these abilities would completely disrupt the system, to the detriment of both predators and prey. Considering the length of evolutionary time and the movements of animal groups, such situations must have occurred many times. Interbreeding groups having intrinsic methods of controlling their populations could easily weather such problems, and so had a selective advantage over those that lacked them; thus the latter groups were replaced. This becomes more plausible when we consider some of the evidence for intrinsic mechanisms of population control.

Territoriality is certainly one of these intrinsic population control mechanisms. There are territorial insects, fish, amphibians, reptiles, birds, and mammals, including man. Dispersal mechanisms are another means of reducing local populations, and if suitable habitats are not found by the dispersing organisms, they perish. Dispersion has the further advantage of assuring that all habitable areas attainable are occupied. Dispersion resulting from population pressure occurs among insects such as the migratory red locusts *(Schistocerca gregaria)* of Africa. It also occurs among muskrats *(Ondatra zibethica)*, lemmings (three genera occur in North America: *Lemmus, Dicrostonyx,* and *Synaptomys*) and probably among humans. Changes in the behavior of the Norway rat in dense populations prevent population increases (Calhoun, 1962). At high densities wild snowshoe hares die of *shock disease* (Green and Larson, 1938). Shock disease is related to the *general adaptation syndrome* (Christian, 1950; Selye, 1956). It involves a breakdown of the adrenal cortex–anterior pituitary system of a vertebrate.

Although this has been only a very sketchy review of the evidence for intrinsic mechanisms of population control, it suggests that they do function in some species. Future research will probably show them to be very widespread. One hopes that man can avoid ruthless control of his population through "natural" means, whether intrinsic or extrinsic, and instead substitute humane, intelligent, alternative mechanisms.

Because we are now the dominant species in virtually all ecosystems on earth, it is necessary to explore our own nature to help us understand our ecological prospects. Eibl-Eibesfeldt's (1970, pp. 446–450) summary of experiments carried out by S. Milgram will help you explore your own nature. These experiments deal with controlled scientific studies of what terrible things good people may do when an authority figure tells them they must. A Chinese proverb is pertinent: "To have principles, first have courage."

SUGGESTED DISCUSSION MATERIAL

1. Where does aesthetic appreciation fit into conservation and ecology? Can it be ignored?

2. In the light of reasonably anticipated needs, what ecological base data should be collected where you live? Have any agencies or individuals attempted to collect such data? Where are they found? What, if anything should be done about this situation?

3. What examples of biotic succession can you find on your campus or in your neighborhood? Can you determine what initiated them? How are human factors determining their course?

4. Discuss biotic diversity. How can it be measured? Do humans live as parts of ecosystems? Or are humans external to ecosystems and just extract materials from them? What are the ecological implications of looking at ecosystems in these two ways? Especially, what are the implications relative to diversity and productivity?

5. Culture is a thin veneer on the mammal called human. Explore the evidence for and against this statement. If it is correct, what should be done to secure man's future? If it is incorrect, why is the world as it is, and what should be done to secure man's future? Relate what you have learned about ecology in your answers to these questions.

Erosion   3

LAND MANAGEMENT TO PRESERVE AND
ENHANCE CONSERVATION VALUES

The first requirement of proper land management is that it
maintain or enhance the ability of the land to support life. In addition, the
possibilities for future use should be maintained as intact as possible.
Where land use possibilities have been reduced, good land management
attempts to regain them or to develop others that are equally valuable.

EROSION

An understanding of erosion is fundamental to the evaluation of land use
practices. *Erosion* is the natural removal of soil (or other material) from its
present site. Wind and water are the principal agents. The less vegetation
covering the soil, the more likely it is to erode.

We all are taught about erosion, but to feel confident that we can
identify its results is not easy. In a way, the ability to identify erosion is like
the ability to "read sign" of animals in the wild, or the ability to discover
clues in solving a crime. Sherlock Holmes, a Wata or Waliangulu tracker
(member of a tribe in East Africa famous for hunting elephant with bows
and poisoned arrows), and erosion experts practice much the same art.
They learn to observe the significant details and successfully piece them
together to reconstruct what has happened.

If you are able to go out-of-doors and practice observing, you will
become confident and capable of identifying erosion and will improve
your awareness. You will be able to identify the results of conservation sins
where before you just suffered from them. Once you have seen them, you
can do something about them.

Erosion is caused by moving water and by wind. Avalanching snow may tear away soil, and heavy rains may cause slumping, mud slides, falling rocks, and so on. The hoof pressure of animals can bare the soil and, as a result, erosion by wind and water may occur. By carrying soil away from shallow ponds in their stomachs and on their skins, mammals are responsible for the formation of water holes or "pans" in central Africa and probably in many other places (Fig. 2–8). In this way they counteract normal erosion to some extent.

WATER EROSION

A rapidly flowing stream removes materials so that its bed lies below the level of the surrounding land. Try to find for observation a small, gravel-bottomed stream to serve as a laboratory for the study of water erosion. Also, plan to spend the next rainstorm out-of-doors.[1] Select a sloping area of bare soil so that when it rains you can go there and watch what happens. If this is not possible, you can obtain some idea of erosion by experimenting in your kitchen sink or anywhere you can produce flowing water.

Note how the currents in the stream you are observing are deflected by logs and boulders. Look at the gravel in the stream and note where the biggest pieces are, and where the smallest and those of intermediate size are located. Pick up a handful of dirt from near the stream. It usually will have particles of many sizes in it, unless the stream has flooded in the fairly recent past. Compare the sizes of particles in this upland dirt with those you gather in a single grab from the stream bed. Now drop the handful of upland dirt into the stream, which for this test must be fairly clear, and watch what happens to the various particles. The bits of grass, leaves, and sticks float downstream. The fine silt forms a cloudy area in the water and may also be carried far downstream, while the largest rocks may drop almost straight to the bottom. From this it is clear that humus and some clay particles are carried farthest by water, and that the next finest soil particles are carried nearly or just as far. The organic and fine mineral components of soil are the most important for plant growth. The faster and more turbulent the flow, the more solids it can carry. As velocity drops, the larger particles settle out. If we want to prevent soil erosion, we must

---

[1] An excellent land management scientist working for the government of Malawi had a standing order that when it rained most of his staff were to drop everything else and go out to watch what was happening. He even maintained a special Land Rover expressly for this purpose. Rain and the resulting erosion were as significant to their training and successful work as fire is to firemen.

prevent the contact of moving water with bare soil, and we must keep water velocities and turbulence as low as possible.

Raindrop erosion

The next step in learning to recognize erosion is to go out in a rainstorm and watch what happens to bare soil on a slope you have selected. What happens when a raindrop strikes the wet soil surface? If events are taking place too fast for you to be sure, hold your hands near the soil surface for a few moments. Now rub your hands together. How did the mud and grit get on them?

The raindrop erosion you have just witnessed does three things. It physically splatters soil particles around, loosening them from others and so allowing them to be carried away more easily by water moving across the surface of the soil. In doing so each drop also moves more soil downhill than uphill. Because of the angle at which it strikes the slope, its bounce away from the slope after striking is in a generally downhill direction. It also tends to pack the very fine particles in clayey soils. Once these pack, they form a waterproof layer in the top few millimeters of the soil surface. This *puddling* forces the rainwater to move across the soil surface, carrying away many surface particles, especially fine ones. Soils high in humus and with plenty of vegetable matter on their surfaces are very resistant to puddling. Soils lacking humus, such as those occurring over large areas of the tropics and in the world's desert areas, are extremely susceptible to puddling, especially if they are the potentially more fertile ones high in clay and low in sand and gravel. Pure sands, of course, can absorb almost any amount of rain with little or no runoff.

Now look for small pebbles or sticks on the surface of the bare soil. If it has been raining hard for a while, or if this bare soil has received heavy rain previously, you may notice that each pebble or stick stands on a small pedestal of soil (Fig. 3–1). The pebble protects the soil immediately below it from the impact of the raindrops. As a result, when water moves across the soil surface, the soil under the pebble resists erosion because of its undisturbed structure. Soil structure is important. Soils with a good nutlike physical structure are said to have good *tilth.* Such soils are usually excellent for plant growth. An important aspect of soil management is the maintenance of optimum physical structure, and protection from erosion is a necessary means toward this end.

Sheet, rill, and gully erosion

Look closely where water is moving across the bare soil as the rain continues. You should be able to see a sorting of the soil particles by size, just

Figure 3–1. Pebbles perched on soil pedestals are evidence of raindrop and sheet erosion.

as you saw in the stream. The only difference is that particle size will be much smaller.

You will see places where water is moving as a thin sheet across the soil, and others where it deepens into rivulets. *Sheet erosion* carries very fine soil particles and humus with it. Rivulets move larger particles also, and deepen by the processes known as *rill* and *gully erosion.* The smallest rivulet in a channel works on the same principles as erosion in a 30-foot-deep gully. Both sheet erosion and gully erosion can become severe (Figs. 3–2 and 3–3).

As you can see in Fig. 3–2, a tree may serve to protect soil. In this case in Malawi, sheet erosion has left pedestals 3–5 feet in height. In East Africa pedestals more than 6 feet high have been observed under trees. This means that at least 6 feet of topsoil has been removed; and much worse cases have been reported.

Gully erosion as shown in Fig. 3–3 progresses uphill. As you watch the rain on the bare soil, look for a place in a rivulet where water is flowing over a lip of less erodible material. Here the water swirls back under the lip and undercuts it. As the undercut headwall moves uphill, the lip weakens and falls away. As it moves, the gully deepends. This is *headwall erosion.*

Figure 3–2. Pedestal under small tree in Malawi, evidence
of severe raindrop and sheet erosion.

Gullies are dramatic. Almost anyone notices large ones; it is the small
ones that many people overlook. Only specialists seem to recognize sheet
erosion except in its most violent forms. Yet sheet erosion probably causes
the greatest losses of soil fertility worldwide. By the time noticeable gully
erosion occurs, sheet erosion has removed the most valuable upper soil
layers. This loss drastically limits land use possibilities for us and for our
descendants. It may take hundreds, and in severe cases thousands, of years
to replace the soil through natural soil-forming processes.

Watch the soil being removed by sheet erosion. Velocities are often
low, so mostly fine material and humus are washed away. Now remembering what you saw in the stream, if the fine particles are removed,
leaving the larger ones, the soil will become progressively more rocky.
Eventually, if there are any pebbles and rocks in the soil, the surface will
become covered by them. The cobblestonelike ground covering is known
as *erosion pavement* (Fig. 3–4).

In some parts of Germany, grapes are grown on steep slopes. Many
of these slopes are far too steep to cultivate with ordinary farm equipment,
including conventional animal-drawn machinery. In one area the ground

Figure 3–3. Severe gully erosion in southwestern Humboldt County, California. Excessive livestock grazing is probably responsible.

is covered with a layer of flat, grayish shale pebbles. Since these slopes have produced wine grapes for several hundred years, some kind of erosion–soil compromise must have been reached. It is likely that the soil is rich in shale, that shale underlies it, and that this rock decomposes very readily. The erosion pavement of flat pebbles may serve as a roof to shed the gentle rains of this region. In this case, the fact that pebbles and rocks cover the soil surfaces is not proof that good conservation practices are being ignored.

The presence of shallow rocky soils can also result from *colluvial soil formation,* as when landslides occur. It can also be at least partly the result of volcanism, as in Fig. 3–5 (Tehama County, California). These boulders probably were transported here in a late Pliocene volcanic mud flow about

Figure 3–4. Extremely severe erosion pavement probably now lying under the waters of Lake Kariba, a man-made lake on the Zambesi River. The larger rocks lie in the areas of highest water velocity during tropical downpours. Compare with Fig. 3–5.

1–2 million years ago. They are mostly composed of andesite, a rock quite resistant to weathering. Both the size of the boulders and sheet erosion have resulted in their still lying above the soil today. In this case it is debatable whether or not these boulders would still be visible in the absence of accelerated sheet erosion. There is little doubt that the smaller stones would now lie below the soil surface if accelerated sheet erosion had not washed the soil away.

Stream turbidity

Change in the turbidity of streams is one of the indications of water erosion on a watershed, but even here caution in interpretation is necessary. In southeastern Alaska, during cold, rainy weather, the waters of the Taku River are quite turbid, as it is a geologically young river. When the sun comes out and there have been 2 or 3 days of warm summer weather, the river near its mouth becomes far more turbid and may rise a foot or more. Why? Because in that area the Taku receives water from glacial melting, and glaciers melt faster in hot weather than they do during cool rains. During these periods of increased turbidity, the water appears milky. This *glacial milk* is caused by finely ground rock particles in suspension.

This example shows that increased rainfall does not necessarily increase stream turbidity, and that turbid waters are not necessarily unnatural. However, in most pristine streams not fed by glaciers, turbidity increases very little with increased stream flow.

During a long period of extremely heavy rain in 1956, Old Tom's Creek, in southeastern Alaska, nearly overran its banks. The water carried leaves, sticks, and bark, but the bottom could still be seen through 4 or 5 feet of water. The watershed was completely soaked, so runoff had to occur. In spite of this, the humus and rooted vegetation successfully protected the watershed and the stream banks (Fig. 3–6). This is the way most streams and their watersheds would behave under heavy rainfall if properly cared for.

How does your study stream look after several days of heavy rain? If it is still running clear, cherish and protect it. It is a rare stream indeed.

Figure 3–5. Volcanic boulder field in Tehama County, California. Compare with Fig. 3–4.

Figure 3–6. Cabin at Old Tom's Creek, southeastern Alaska, set in a virgin forest. This salmon stream has flowed over the land in the foreground, as the vegetation shows. Although it nearly overran its banks by the cabin, it still flowed clear except for the leaves, needles, and sticks picked up from the banks.

WIND EROSION

The same principles that apply to water erosion also apply to wind erosion. A vigorously growing vegetative cover is the best protection. In each case it is the valuable humus and the fine materials that are lost most readily when vegetative cover is reduced or removed. Porous soils are strikingly different in their resistance to wind and water erosion. Because of their ability to absorb rain and runoff water they are very resistant to water erosion, but unfortunately they are not exceptionally resistant to wind erosion. In general, wind erosion is most important in areas with long dry periods, such as many of the wheat-growing regions of the world.

Wind erosion and wildlife

At one time the big game herds of the Wankie National Park area in Rhodesia moved in with the coming of the rains and departed when the temporary pans dried. With the establishment of permanent water sources in the park, these movements have largely stopped. Most of the animals remain in the park, where they are readily visible to tourists and are protected from hunting. The windmills that pump water into the permanent pans are protected from itchy elephants by small dry moats.

Under protection, the now more sedentary herds increased rapidly and began to damage severely their own range by overutilizing and trampling the vegetation. Before 1959 wind erosion had already started around some of the pans (Figs. 3–7 and 3–8). The surface of the sandy soil showed wind-caused ripple marks, just as though it were the beach of an ocean, lake, or large river.

Interestingly enough, the sandy soils in much of Wankie National Park are considered to be *aeolian* (wind-deposited) sands. They lie in ridges all oriented in about the same direction, former sand dunes shaped by winds during an earlier dry period. With human mismanagement of wildlife, this process started again.

Fortunately, steps were taken to correct the situation by stopping some of the windmills. The temporarily dry pans no longer attract wildlife in great numbers. They are left dry just long enough for vegetation to cover the soil around them again. In the tropics this happens much faster than in colder climates. In addition, fairly large numbers of elephants and some other species have been removed to lessen pressure on the vegetation. This is apparently necessary in the absence of human hunting. Man and wildlife evolved together in Africa, and man is biologically a hunter. Without his hunting some species increase too greatly and damage both their own habitat and that of other species.

Figure 3–7. Active wind erosion at Ngamo Pan, Wankie National Park, Rhodesia, in 1959. Too frequent fires and yearround use by excessive numbers of animals were probably responsible.

Figure 3–8. African buffalo, *Syncerus caffer*, approaching Ngamo Pan in Wankie National Park, Rhodesia, during 1959. The extensive bare ground had undergone wind erosion. Great amounts of animal dung were present in this flat sandy soil. Such soils should revegetate rapidly when animal pressure is reduced. Also see Fig. 3–7.

Wind erosion, domestic stock, and recreation

In northern California there is a sand dune area along the ocean shore near McKinleyville. These dunes are relatively small and are stabilized inland by bush lupine *(Lupinus arboreus)* and some hardy grasses, including one introduced from Europe for the purpose *(Ammophila arenaria)*. The dunes near the coast will probably exist for a long time, because the pounding surf of winter storms will guarantee a wide beach free of rooted vegetation.

Ten miles farther south there is a dune area south of the Mad River. Here the dunes are larger. These dunes were stabilized but are growing again. Recreationists driving dune buggies and motorcycles over them are destroying the vegetation (Fig. 3–9). These dunes are now moving inland, engulfing the small remaining stands of a unique forest (Fig. 3–10). Three or four miles farther south, and for largely the same reasons, dunes are starting to engulf the small town of Manila (Figs. 3–11 and 3–12).

Wind erosion caused by mismanagement of livestock can be seen near Winnemucca, Nevada (Fig. 3–13). Here in a very dry area, dune formation is active. South of Cape Mendocino in coastal Humboldt County, California, is another shocking example of wind erosion and dune formation caused by domestic stock. Livestock has also increased dune formation near the Mad River, where the damage is being intensified by dune buggy and motorcycle recreationists.

Much of this mismanagement involves private lands. The California and Nevada livestock owners mentioned above are breaking no laws. Yet what options are they leaving for those that follow them? Sand dunes feed few humans. It will not be long before obvious need will force a change in our legal rights as landowners. Such treatment of our environment is immoral. It is time ranchers who practice good land management put effective pressure on their despoiling colleagues. If they do not, someone less understanding probably will.

Figure 3–9. Dune buggies near Arcata, California, July 1971. These vehicles and motorcycles damage the fragile dune vegetation. With the death of the plants, the dunes advance and overwhelm other biotic communities. Compare with Figs. 3–10, 3–11, and 3–12.

Figure 3–10. Dead pine killed by advancing sand near Arcata, California. This tree can be seen in the upper left corner of Fig. 3–9. The dunes are encroaching on the pine forest in the background.

Figure 3–11. Coastal sand dune endangering a small farm near Manila, California. Dune vegetation cannot withstand heavy grazing pressure and still retain the vigor needed to survive the effects of blowing sand.

Figure 3–12. Sand dunes endangering Manila, California. The beer and soft drink cans are typical litter along this beautiful coast.

Figure 3–13. Moving dunes near Winnemucca, Nevada. Excessive grazing by domestic stock is probably responsible.

Results of wind erosion

Indications of past wind erosion include erosion pavement and a difference in ground level at fence lines or at other breaks in the topography. These are also indications of water erosion; perhaps one or both may be responsible. Ripple marks on bare soil surfaces in flat areas and the accumulation of loose soil particles in animal tracks or other depressions are good indicators of wind erosion (Fig. 3–14).

In any consideration of erosion it is important to note that some erosion is natural. The deep, rich *loess* soils along the upper Mississippi River, for example, were deposited by winds. They are derived from fine rock particles scoured from rock by ice during the Wisconsin glaciation. What we must worry about is accelerated erosion which removes the fertile *A horizon* faster than it is formed. This is the sort of erosion that occurred on a vast scale in the Dust Bowl.

Figure 3–14. Severe sheet and wind erosion on a private cattle ranch in the Limpopo Intensive Conservation Area, Rhodesia. Note how loose dust covers the soil surface, and also that the exposed stones have had soil eroded from around them. About 6 years before this photograph was taken, this area is said to have supported a rich grass cover. The cattle-ranching enterprise dates from that time.

SUGGESTED DISCUSSION MATERIAL

1. Read soils literature as a background for a discussion of the relationships between soil fertility and erodibility. How could this knowledge be applied to prevention and control of soil erosion.

2. What are the long-term implications of irrigation as a farming method? Investigate the literature concerning the movement of salts in soils and the movement of fertilizer and pesticide components. What human health considerations are related to the formation and movement of nitrates and other materials in and through irrigated soils? Where is water for irrigation obtained? How much does it really cost, and who pays for it? Where does the water go? What are the social and ecological implications? What could be done about any problems you discover?

3. Explore the various governmental assistance plans for measures related to water, wind, and soil management on private lands. Do they ever seem to work at cross-purposes? Where does the money come from to support them? Are they effective in achieving reasonable goals as judged from a conservation standpoint? Are they more available to farms of a certain size or value than to others? What are the long-term social effects of these programs? Can or should anything be done about them, and, if so, what?

4. Discuss the pros and cons of natural and synthetic fertilizers. Consider the energy uses involved. Relate your discussion to farming enterprises ranging in size from small peasant holdings to large commercial company or cooperative farms.

Land Use   4

RANGE LANDS

In evaluating range lands, range managers record range *condition* and *trend*. Range condition is the present status of the range, which may be given in descriptive terms or as a numerical rating. Trend indicates whether or not the condition of the range is improving. Both are necessary to evaluate current and future use. If the trend is toward more bare soil, it is generally acknowledged that destocking is required. Fortunately, this is not necessarily true in all cases.

Destocking

Much more is involved in animal–range relationships than simply animal numbers. Partial destocking as a panacea for reversing range deterioration has unfortunately resulted in range mismanagement. People thought that by reducing the *stocking rate* they had solved the problem, and were then amazed to realize later that deterioration had continued. For years we have failed to ask the right questions in our studies of animal–range relationships. The key to all research is asking significant questions.

Grazing and browsing by animals can affect a range in complex ways (Figs. 4–1 and 4–2). Selective grazing (even goats are very selective, given the opportunity) favors some plants over others in interspecific and intraspecific competition. Animals may use a single plant at different times and in different ways. Some animals have almost no effect on plants; for example, steenbuck *(Raphicerus campestris)* may eat leaves or blossoms that have fallen from trees. Others may have drastic effects; for example, an elephant *(Loxodonta africana)* may push over an acacia and munch off the exposed roots. The same elephant may also eat the nutritious pods of

Figure 4–1. Browse lines on trees in the Urungwe area of Rhodesia.
Dead trees, the "weeds" that look like rank grass in the foreground, and the
lack of young trees are all signs of land misuse. Fire and excessive animal
numbers, especially of African buffalo, are probably responsible. This photograph was taken in 1961.

Acacia albida. These pods even serve as an emergency food for man.
Later some of the seeds that pass through the elephant will germinate and
grow in his dung—if a guinea fowl *(Numida meleagris)* does not kick apart
the droppings, find the seeds, and eat them first. The droppings of the
elephant and those of other herbivores fertilize the ground and provide
humus. The urine of these animals returns nitrogen to the soil. So in a
balanced healthy rangeland situation, there is an exceedingly complex
meshwork of interacting factors which ensures the health and dynamic
stability (homeostasis) of the ecosystem.

Time factors and intensity of grazing

One factor in animal management on extensive rangelands that has until
recently been inadequately considered is the interrelationship between the
intensity of grazing and the time or times at which it takes place. Recent
clipping studies and other pasture research in England, South Africa, and
elsewhere have yielded worthwhile insights into these relationships. If the

Figure 4–2. A *Ceanothus* species hedged by black-tailed deer on King's Peak in southwestern Humboldt County, California. Such shapes are indicative of heavy browsing pressure, as is the very unpalatable sticky-leaved forb, yerba santa, *Eriodictyon californicum*, which can be seen in the foreground. This photograph was taken in 1967.

American bison *(Bison bison)* had not been nearly exterminated, we probably would have gained this understanding far sooner. Someone would have wondered how such large populations could be supported without damaging the range. Migratory patterns were probably the reason. A ranching consultant in southern Africa has improved range conditions by *increasing the stocking rate* of cattle. This was achieved by insightful manipulation of animal densities and duration of grazing relative to the ecological characteristics of the grazing areas. In some cases stocking rates have had to be increased as much as fivefold (Anonymous, 1971a, b).

Two major factors are involved in this kind of management: effects on the vegetation and effects on the soil. Cattle hoof pressure is used to cultivate soil and plant the seeds of desirable species. When a desirable species or set of species is ready to seed, cattle *(Bos taurus)* are brought in for a few days at an extremely high stocking rate. Their trampling churns the surface of the soil, providing a seedbed for the desired plants. The cattle are then removed before they cause deleterious soil compaction.

The principle can be explained in several ways. One way is to think of the sheepfoot rollers used to pack roadbeds and dam fills. In passing over an area the first few times, they churn up the surface soil. If they are then removed, there is some deep compaction, but the upper 2–3 feet are very loose. If this area is used as a seedbed, the deep roots of perennial grasses soon penetrate and break up the deep compaction, and a rich vegetative cover can be established. This is essentially what short-term high-intensity stocking of cattle achieves. Is this not reminiscent of what must have happened as great dark herds of bison migrated across the plains?

The effects of time can also be explained another way. Twice each day, an African woman takes her water pot, walks to a stream, fills the pot, and walks back home with it balanced gracefully on her head. A leafy twig rests on top to reduce slopping. If her village were to be abandoned, her path would still be visible, sometimes for a year or two afterward. Now suppose 365 women walk single file to the stream and return with water twice in 1 day, but not thereafter. Their trail would probably be almost impossible to see in a week or two during the growing season, and it would be visible not much longer than that during the dry season.

By stocking very intensely for short periods carefully adjusted for a specific area, cattle can be made to eat as if they were a whole spectrum of herbivorous species. They simulate the grazing effects of a dense mul-tispecies herbivore community. When first put into a pasture, cattle eat the most palatable plants, the ones that American range managers have called "ice cream plants." They then eat the less and less palatable, finally feeding on the very unpalatable ones. As long as there are no toxic plants, and as long as this period of eating the unpalatable ones is short, the cattle do not suffer weight loss. Cattle on such short-duration, high-intensity grazing may gain weight while cattle on adjacent ranches lose weight.

Forcing cattle to eat unpalatable plants prevents these plants from obtaining a competitive advantage over palatable species. To decrease the unpalatable plants and increase the palatable ones most efficiently requires expert consideration of both time of year and intensity, frequency, and duration of feeding pressure.

Natural grazing systems

It is now becoming clear that the idea of a *sacrifice area* around waterholes or other places of stock concentration is essentially wrong. With proper management it is possible to have grass right to the edges of waterholes. This is of great interest in the management of wildlife both alone and in combination with domestic stock. We have only begun to learn how herbivore productivity works in natural areas, and how we can increase the productivity of wildlife species through sophisticated management techniques. We must learn how natural grazing systems work before we lose them. Because of the urgent need for animal protein, we need to experiment with wildlife management techniques as imaginative and sophisticated as the cattle management techniques we have discussed. If such methods are possible with cattle, what might be possible with other species alone and in combination?

The present world shortage of animal protein will worsen very rapidly as populations continue to increase. We already desperately need to know how to produce more animal protein; and even if the predicted massive famines do occur and eliminate many people, we will still need to know. It is a virtual certainty that we can produce far more animal protein with both domestic animals and wildlife than with either alone. Vast areas of all continents cannot be successfully used for agricultural field crops, so production of animal protein will probably continue to be the most important human use of such areas.

WATERSHEDS AND MULTIPLE USE

Range lands are also important as watersheds and often produce forests and recreational opportunities as well. There is a tendency to think in terms of a single use for which a given parcel of land is best suited. Seldom is this realistic, because many uses are made of almost all lands. The dedication of land to a single use is appropriate only when extremely rare or delicate biotas are involved, or when historical, scientific, or aesthetically valuable phenomena must be strictly protected from almost all human entry—where we must follow the admonition, "Look but don't touch." Just as lands principally used for domestic livestock production have other subsidiary uses, so watersheds usually can produce more than water.

In a small and very land-poor country in Africa, several low-quality forest areas have been kept as watersheds. This is essentially their only use, yet they have been managed as if for lumbering. The result of such management is rather poor watershed protection and no worthwhile forest or anything else such as wildlife habitat or rangeland for domestic stock. These areas could probably serve as far better watersheds if they had fewer trees and more and richer grass. They could also support much more wildlife and, under careful management, fair numbers of domestic stock as well. They could do this while producing very nearly as much useful wood as when managed as if to grow trees for lumbering. Certainly, the overall value as a watershed could be enhanced while adding one or more important uses. This example shows the need for an ecological approach to land management.

In Lake County, California, at the Hopland Research Station, studies of small-watershed management have been carried out over several years. They have clearly shown that spring and stream flow can be greatly augmented and the duration of flow increased by removing from the watershed trees such as oaks (*Quercus* spp.) and willows (*Salix* spp.).

If a watershed is paved, as has been done on Gibraltar, even more of the rainfall can be collected. Paving is probably legitimate where every possible drop of water must be collected for uses such as human, stock, or wildlife drinking water. But just as a paved watershed yields nothing but water, so a treeless one loses all those assets contributed by trees. Decisions about the kind of watershed we maintain must rest on a balancing of values. We should always remember that a watershed's productivity must be protected as much as possible and if possible enhanced, and that it is necessary to leave ourselves options for the future. It takes 250 years to grow a really nice, big oak which produces lots of acorns, shade for cattle, deer, and humans, and nest sites for birds. Even 20-year-old oaks do not do the job nearly so well—and 20 years is one human generation. One should think carefully before cutting down old oaks to gain a little more spring flow.

FOREST LANDS

The U.S. Forest Service administers the national forests. Some of this land is completely devoid of trees, so it is obvious that management of wood production must be only one of the jobs of the U.S. Forest Service. It is for this reason that specialists in range, wildlife, and fisheries management, among others, are required in this organization if it is to manage its land properly. Even at the very best sites for timber growth, there are other things that go on in addition to the rapid growth of trees. In fact, in some cases these sites may even be so valuable for other uses that these uses should take precedence over timber production.

One of the great problems involved in the commercial production of timber is that all efforts to regenerate forests after cutting depend on predictions of timber need at the time the trees will mature. Perhaps this realization has been partly responsible for the frequently belated and often merely token efforts of the lumbering industry to reestablish the forests they have removed. How does one know whether or not there will be a demand for a particular type of timber 30, 60, or 80 years from the present?

We do know that natural forests have great aesthetic appeal. This tends to be lost on most of the people living in such forests, especially those who hear cash registers ringing when they look at a well-formed tree.

The coastal redwood forest

It is doubtful that a forest more impressive and aesthetically appealing than the mature coastal redwoods *(Sequoia sempervirens)* exists anywhere in the world. We have preserved such a miserably small remnant because this forest probably pays a logger more for his effort than does any other. We do need lumber, but we certainly have not needed and do not need to fell as much of the virgin coastal redwoods as has already been cut (see page 142). We have lost the opportunity to experience the immenseness of a virgin redwood forest, not the height and bulk of individual trees, but the aggregate of thousands of timbered acres. We can still look at them somewhat as we can look at a Winslow Homer seascape, and they are beautiful and moving. But, this is not a virgin forest, just as a Winslow Homer seascape is not the sea.

The world's people have lost this opportunity for at least the next 1200 years, because it takes that long to grow a mature coastal redwood forest (Fig. 4–3). At 20 years for a human generation, that is 60 human generations.[1] Can you reckon that far back in your genealogy? Can you trace back even one-quarter as far—15 generations? For its personal enrichment the lumber industry has successfully fought attempts over many years to save a significant part of the coastal redwood forests. Now we have a Redwood National Park which is really a tattered series of forest remnants strung sparsely on a thread of clear-cut and burned landscape. Only in our minds can we or the next 60 generations of humans see the vast, powerful, green forest. Is it worth it? How will our great-great-grandchildren answer that question? We can only speculate; but we have eliminated one of their options.

The coastal redwood forest is just one very unfortunate case. There are forests in many other parts of the world, especially in the tropics, that are in great danger at this moment. Many of the same companies are involved. Like the redwoods these forests are valuable not only for lumber and for the aesthetic experiences they provide, but are also of great potential value for scientific study. We can only guess what benefits such investigations could yield. Opportunities for such studies are much reduced when the size of these areas is decreased so that edge effects extend significantly throughout the forest. It is already too late to study the coastal redwood forest successfully for this reason. This does not mean that no studies should be made of it, only that it is no longer possible to study an unaltered virgin redwood forest. The effects associated with the forest's edge now permeate throughout.

---

[1]It is worth noting that a 2000-year-old redwood alive in 1970 was already 1330 years old at the beginning of the fourteenth century, about the time gunpowder was invented and still nearly two centuries before Columbus discovered America.

Figure 4–3. Sign near Redwood National Park in Humboldt County, California. "Overmature" is the lumber industry's term for virgin. The sign is honest but misleading. Because of the very low germination rate of coastal redwood seeds, the seedlings produced will be largely spruce and Douglas fir. Redwood regeneration will probably come largely from stump sprouts. In 1200 years, or perhaps longer, another mature redwood forest may exist here. In fighting the establishment of Redwood National Park, the lumber industry posted another honest but misleading sign saying that the number of redwoods alive today is greater than ever. Most of these are seedlings and saplings, including the stump sprouts. This is not obvious to the unsuspecting public, most of whom lack any concept of the vast amount of time it takes to grow a mature redwood. Although 100 seedlings can grow in the space occupied by a single virgin redwood stump, only 1 can attain full maturity.

Some forest assets

Forests, in addition to their aesthetic and scientific aspects, serve many other purposes. For example, they protect watersheds. The surface under even an 80-year-old, second-growth redwood forest acts almost like a sponge. You can pour a bucket of water onto it and almost as fast as you can pour, it soaks into the surface. Some of the water falling on the watershed is transpired by the trees, but their roots anchor the soil, and their leaves intercept the rain and reduce its impact on the ground. The litter of leaves and twigs on the ground forms a rich mat called *duff.*

Forests also provide some food for domestic stock, and food and shelter for wildlife. Wildlife, by increasing diversity, help to protect a natural forest from an excessive increase in species deleterious to the forest and to the species within it. In not every case has diversity been sufficient to protect certain forest species from drastic losses, such as those caused in North America by Dutch elm disease and chestnut blight. These, of course, were both imported by man, and the elms and chestnuts here had not evolved the necessary resistance to them as had those in Europe. But as a rule, forest mammals, birds, predatory insects, and so on have a great deal to do with the stability of the forest as an entity. The *stability principle* states that, the more diverse the biota, the more stable a community tends to be (see page 35). The maintenance of biotic diversity should be one of the aims of a land manager.

Dangers of monoculture

A forestry method that has been practiced for about the last 50 years is the planting of large even-aged stands of a single tree species. As a result, insect attacks sometimes become a problem. A recent example occurred in Malawi where extensive stands of a Mexican pine *(Pinus patula)* were planted, creating an exotic pine monoculture. In the Dedza area a grasshopper that formerly lived on other types of plants has now developed a taste for the Mexican pine. Some ecologists anticipate serious trouble should this grasshopper increase drastically in numbers on its new food source. Similar problems are encountered in the cultivation of any crop. But trees are unlike most domestic crops in that they stay in the same place and at the same density for many years, giving insects and other possible pests an opportunity to produce genetic variants that excellently fit the extensive, newly created niche. With the usual rotation of crops and the annual removal of plant material, or at least its plowing under as *green manure,* opportunities for pests are reduced in normal agriculture. Thus in spite of the seeming logic of growing trees like any other row crop, there are serious potential flaws in the technique. The likelihood of pest problems is one; aesthetic impoverishment is another.

FARM LANDS

The corporate farm

The ideals of manufacturing efficiency have been applied to farming in North America. A farm is considered in the same light as a factory and, in order to achieve comparable kinds of financial efficiency, it is essential to invest very heavily in the land and also in the equipment and supplies required to produce a crop. Crop output is measured against the yardstick of profit and loss, with all effort made to maximize profit. As in manufacturing, profit increases relative to the cost to produce a unit commodity as the enterprise increases in size. At a certain limiting size, so-called bureaucratic inefficiencies start to reduce the percentage profit per unit produced. Such inefficiencies are reduced by mechanisms that simplify the operation, allowing closer control by fewer administrative personnel. One way to do this in a farming operation is to increase the size of the fields; another is to decrease the variety of crops produced. The latter holds the danger that the crop may face a depressed market in any particular year. To a large extent this danger has been removed by guaranteed government prices for important farm commodities. Under these circumstances a farm operator knows that he can realize at least the support price for a crop he produces.

The price-support system and the structure of farm taxation were established presumably to protect small family farms. In practice, they have encouraged the growth of massive corporate farming enterprises. From an ecological and aesthetic point of view this is not good. It even has had unfortunate sociological effects, if one feels there was something worthwhile in farm life on family-owned home farms which corporate farms have largely replaced.

Farming evaluation

There are legitimate ways other than by profit-and-loss accounting to evaluate the success of a farming technique, and one of these is in terms of the amount and nutritional quality of food that finds its way into the stomachs of people. This is seldom the same as the amount harvested from the land, and it may have only a casual relationship to profit and loss of the usual kind. We should evaluate food production also in energy terms, calculating the energy used to produce and get food to the mouth of the consumer. In the case of factory farms, in the U.S.A., this should include such unexpected items as all legal fees and all the fossil energy used. We should even include the proportionate energy costs of agricultural research, of handling income tax money for farm price support, and certainly the costs of family automobile trips to the grocery and of operating family refrigerators.

Peasant agriculture in some cases may produce at least as much harvestable food per acre as does modern mechanized agriculture. If true energy costs are considered, the mechanized farm and marketing structure of food production and distribution in developed countries cannot compete with peasant agriculture. This is why countries densely settled by peasant agriculturalists cannot industralize unless assisted by others who supply them with food or who help them expand their energy base. This expansion still requires the use of fossil fuel, geothermal power, or nuclear power. All cause unfortunate amounts of pollution.

From a conservation point of view, the important consideration is that the ability of the earth to produce the foods, materials, and intangibles needed by man not be lost and, if possible, that it be enhanced. Among the intangibles required by mankind is the opportunity to make choices. This means that in the cropping of farmland it is essential that the soil be protected. In general, row crops are the most damaging to the soil, and in the most arid parts of the earth the effects of farming tend to be most damaging. Many sites should never be cleared for conventional farming. These include steep hillsides, and in more arid regions even flatlands.

Research on erosion losses caused by maize *(Zea mays)* farming in Rhodesia has been conducted at the Henderson Research Station near Salisbury. By intensive nitrogen fertilization, by chopping and plowing under stalks and foliage, and by planting maize broadcast as one might plant grass, high yields per acre were achieved with practically no soil loss in excess of normal geological erosion (Figs. 4–4 and 4–5).

Figure 4–4. The experimental plots above these soil collection tanks were planted with the maize seen in the photograph. Such studies have shown that very high yields of maize can be obtained from such gentle slopes, while little erosion occurs and the fertility and tilth of the soil are maintained.

Figure 4–5. At the Henderson Research Station near Salisbury, Rhodesia, these devices trap soil washed from experimental plots located above them on the slope.

Such innovations will probably be accepted slowly if at all. For peasant agriculture it requires capital investment which often is not feasible. In agriculturally mechanized countries machinery is designed for maize grown as a row crop. It will probably be a long while before farmers are prepared to try growing it in any other way. As it is presently grown, maize is one of the crops that is very hard on the soil, but apparently it need not be. The habit of underplanting maize with squash or similar crops, as practiced by peasant agriculturalists, results in increased soil protection. Attempts to discourage this practice should be discontinued.

Swidden agriculture

The swidden or cut-and-burn agriculture practiced in the tropics successfully carries such soil protection processes much farther, and the result on soils subject to laterization is desirable when excessive population does not force abuse of the method (Geertz, 1963). As many as 40 different crop plant species may be grown in a 3-acre swidden plot in the Philippines. The timing of planting, the position in the plot, and the type of crop, from root crops through grain crops to tree crops, are all carefully determined by competent agriculturalists. Such complexity mimics the natural complexity of tropical forests, and many advantages result for the farmer and for the land. No lasting decrease in the land's ability to support man occurs if the fallow periods are sufficiently long.

Paddy rice

In Indonesia the other principal method of agriculture is paddy culture of rice, that is, the growing of rice in shallow water for at least part of the growth period. Here also the methods employed by traditional agriculturalists have resulted in the ability of wet-rice fields to produce adequate crops for centuries. Some of the irrigation systems are known to be about 1400 years old. It is surprising how greatly the yield of wet rice can be increased by more intensive farming methods. These labor-intensive advances in farming techniques have resulted in greater employment and more food for the exploding Javanese population. Geertz (1963) feels that the two types of agriculture, swidden and wet-rice, lie at the root of the uneven population distribution and the inescapable social and cultural perplexities that have resulted. Swidden agriculture requires dispersed, stabilized populations of relatively mobile people. By contrast, yields from wet-rice culture can expand to support and employ increasing populations of sedentary cultivators. Of course there is a limit to the size of population that can be supported, and that limit is being approached. In fact, there is concern that technical improvements, such as fertilization of wet rice, employed with disregard for the psychological, social, and cultural implications will aggravate the difficulties they were meant to alleviate (Geertz, 1963).

The "green revolution"

New, high-yielding varieties of rice and wheat have recently been developed, and planted in several countries. Their introduction coincided with good weather following two drought years, and production has been substantial. This is being called the green revolution, and the strains involved are termed "wonder crops." Paddock (1970), a consultant in tropical agriculture, is less than enthusiastic. He says, "When there is such a thing as a Green Revolution, its name will be disaster if it arrives ahead of a Population Revolution." Norman E. Borlaug received a Nobel Prize in 1970 for his success in breeding these high-yielding varieties. He also is worried about the world population problem and considers these food crops only a means to keep people alive while human population control is being achieved.

A strain of hybrid maize much higher yielding than local varieties is cultivated in Malawi. After the ears ripen the Africans store them in large bins woven of twigs. A species of weevil (order Coleoptera) infests the maize and eats its way through the kernels. The weevil prefers the hybrid maize. As the people are consuming the maize, so are the weevils. The weevils eat through the hybrid maize so fast that a person can obtain more to eat by growing the local strains rather than the high-yielding hybrid. The proposed solution to this problem was to use metal containers for storage and to dust the stored maize with DDT.

Human consumers will be poisoned by the DDT along with the weevils, and in Malawi it is doubtful that one can very easily introduce store-bought storage bins when one can make his own or at least buy a handmade one by bartering some of the corn that is to be stored in it. Perhaps someone should try breeding a weevil-resistant hybrid maize which is at least the equal of the local strains in nutrient value. Whether or not it yields more on the stalk, it should yield more to the belly, other factors being equal.

In developed countries we feel immune to such problems, but we are not. Much plant breeding contributes just as little to our health and enjoyment of food. For example, it took an Illinois hybrid sweet corn bred for flavor to remind people of what they had already given up in taste to have large, full ears of sweet corn.

Maintaining land productivity

As has been indicated before and will be repeated throughout this book, the ultimate test of man's successful uses of his environment is that those uses allow a maximum number and variety of uses of the same areas by the earth's future inhabitants. In the management of lands for farming or for other purposes, this means that the productivity of the soil must be maintained or improved. A look at farming areas almost anywhere in the world quickly shows how poorly this requirement is being met. Unfortunately, the "wearing out" of farms has been accepted as normal over much of the world. With proper care, land does not wear out, and some soils can be improved.

Almost all "primitive" agriculture practiced before the advent of rapid population increases had some effective means of maintaining the fertility of the soil or of ensuring that fertility would be rejuvenated by natural successional processes (Fig. 4–6). This is true even if we include European peasant agriculture until shortly before the industrial revolution.

Figure 4–6. Recently cleared swidden agricultural land in Rhodesia. The piles of ashes will be scattered and hoed into the ground to prepare the seedbed. When fertility drops too low, the people will leave this land and start another garden elsewhere. With increasing human population, these areas are not allowed to lie fallow long enough for the soil to regain its fertility. Poorer crops and starvation result.

In practically all such societies, there were accepted rules of land inheritance. Thus an owner *knew* that some day he would be handing his farm on to one or more of his children. No man is likely to jeopardize the life of his offspring if he can possibly avoid it. Since these people depended on their own agricultural production to feed themselves, a ruined farm meant possible death by starvation for a farmer and his family.

With an essentially stable population, or one smaller than the potential carrying capacity for peasant agriculturalists, this was feasible. However, when populations increase in such a system, farms must be subdivided, or individuals must emigrate to other lands. Subdivision possibilities are limited by the fact that a certain amount of land is necessary to support a man and his family. With the filling up of the "empty" spaces of the world, the opportunity for emigration was curtailed. The industrial revolution and, more recently, rapid advances in technology and the use of fossil energy sources have provided new opportunities for the ecological equivalent of emigration from farming lands in technologically advanced nations.

Farms have been fused into larger and larger units run by fewer people per acre. Some farms in the U.S.A. have become so huge that they receive more than 1 million dollars each year from the federal government in subsidies. In 1969 the average farm size in the U.S.A. was more than 300 acres (122 hectares).

The processes mentioned in the preceding paragraph are associated with population increase, and have resulted in the scattered garden plots of BaTonga farmers in the Gwembe Valley of south central Africa. They have also led to the large company farms of the Central Valley of California. In each case the result is less personal involvement of farmers in maintaining the productivity of the soil. In the Gwembe Valley a peasant farmer must employ every possible means just to keep from starving each year. Even if he wants to, he cannot think about the future unless he can produce enough to keep himself alive. Famine is common there now, and has been quite common in the past. As time passes, it will probably become more frequent and severe.

On the big farms in the U.S.A., lack of personal interest in the care of the land has a different cause. Here farming is based on economics. Sometimes good care results. It is not difficult to show that farmers practicing good conservation achieve long-run financial gains. The trouble is that finances are seldom handled in terms of the long run. Too often there is an immediate need for extra cash. If the aim is to make money, the faster it is made the quicker it can be reinvested to make more money. Financially, it may well "pay" to wear out a farm and reinvest either in another farm or in some other enterprise. Only when there is a moral feeling for the land, or for someone to whom our land will devolve, will we give land the necessary care. We can and should develop laws requiring proper land husbandry, but as with any laws, they will be effective only if a substantial portion of the people support them. Better than any law is a social consciousness and the pressure of peers to ensure compliance with enlightened social standards of good land husbandry. Best of all would be a combination of the two. We can hardly settle for less.

CITIES, SUBURBS, AND RURAL AREAS

Industrial countries

In industrialized nations cities grow in population, but as people acquire relatively high amounts of material wealth they tend to move to the suburbs or to the nearby country. By doing so they attempt to escape the city while still profiting from its positive aspects. Business and industry follow, or may even lead the exodus in an attempt to attract capable personnel. As a result, the advantages of suburban or rural life are diluted or removed, and the centrifugal movement from population centers continues in a metastasizing cancerous fashion. This process is now accelerating, as it becomes abundantly clear to urban dwellers that our mental and physical health are damaged by life in the cities (Anonymous, 1971c; Gilluly, 1972). The use of transportation powered by fossil fuels and the construction of highways, rail lines, subways, and airports makes this possible. Even in smaller towns with relatively minor amounts of industry, there is a tendency for urban sprawl.

Various remedies have been proposed. The most generally accepted is that cities be made more habitable for man by developing more parks and recreation areas of other kinds and by decreasing air pollution, noise, and so on, that is, by making city life more attractive than country life. However, there may be a large number of people who will give up some conveniences to escape living in even a model city. If this number becomes large relative to the population, then industrialized countries are already severely overpopulated. Perhaps what we need is a propaganda machine of the *Brave New World* type to convince us that life in the city is good for us, so that we can reduce our impact on rural and natural areas.

If a large proportion of the world's population, given the choice and the material resources, elects to live in rural areas, we have ahead of us some rather disturbing times. Certainly, a temporary amelioration can come from making cities more livable, and perhaps also from making the country less livable by a reduction in rural services. The cessation of new highway construction seems to be of first priority in moving toward a reduction in rural services. If the funds saved are then spent on improving life in the city, double value will be received, the cities will become more livable and the rural areas will remain relatively natural. An example would be the use of highway funds to develop high quality, aesthetically and environmentally sound mass transit systems, or to create more urban green spaces to enrich the quality of city life.

Although population distribution patterns have developed haphazardly in the past, we must quickly and intelligently plan future distribution patterns. This will require information not available at present. Thus research in population distribution planning must quickly receive high priority.

Developing countries

In densely populated developing countries, the problem is quite different. There human movement into cities occurs at a very rapid rate. Although some of this movement may be to attain the cultural benefits of cities, much appears to be a direct result of the problem of obtaining enough to eat in rural areas. This movement is aggravated by the importation of food from other regions, because the food arrives first in the large cities. Starving people move as close as possible to the food source, namely, into these cities. Also, in the cities there are greater possibilities for wage earning and other means of acquiring money, hence food. Again the problem is fundamentally one of overpopulation, and the solution will be very difficult in more densely populated countries. It seems unlikely that these problems can be solved without external assistance, and the ability of other countries to provide this assistance is decreasing at an accelerating rate.

In planning the distribution of human populations, we must ask what kinds of distribution patterns will lead to the highest quality existence for those involved, while maintaining as many choices as possible for our descendants. The answers may well be different if the population sizes are different. Huge megalopolises and marine floating city-states may be the only way to save natural areas if populations continue to increase for even a few more years. Under such conditions, natural areas may become psychologically essential for human existence (Iltis, 1970; Weisman, Mann, and Barker, 1965).

FIRE

Devastating wildfire

Many destructive forest fires have swept the timberlands of North America. The famous Tillamook Burn of Oregon occurred in 1933. It was less devastating than the Peshtigo fire of northern Wisconsin, which took place in 1871 at the same time as the famous Chicago fire which "stole its press." The Peshtigo fire killed from 1100 to more than 1400 people, over five times the number dying in Chicago, and caused much more damage than the Chicago fire. However, since the fire was not in a large city, hardly anyone outside the area then or now has ever heard of it (Cantwell, 1970; Wells, 1968).

The more familiar devastating effects of fire are too well known to emphasize. The actual ferocity, the huge, roaring, self-generated winds sweeping into the infernos, and the explosive igniting of whole blocks of trees are so extreme that hardly anyone can really believe them who has not actually witnessed them. For example, "a man . . . saw one of the town's [Peshtigo's] most beautiful girls racing down a blazing [wooden] sidewalk and stopped in her tracks as her streaming blond hair burst into flames. Examining the spot the next day he found two nickel garter buckles and a little mound of white-grey ash" (Cantwell, 1970).

But fire is a normal factor of the environment in many places. Fire is often extremely destructive, but it also can be a benign and useful element of the environment. Sometimes an apparently mild fire or a succession of mild fires can cause lasting damage, while one that appears violent may in fact cause relatively little long-term trouble for the environment (Fig. 4–7).

Tundra fires are not dramatic to see, but because it takes about 50 years for climax lichen vegetation to develop again, their effect on the caribou *(Rangifer tarandus)* that rely on these lichens is drastic. In fact, the combination of natural and increasing man-caused fire and excessive killing has endangered some caribou populations of Canada, thus endangering the people who rely on them for food. From 1961 through 1964 there were known to be 1250 forest fires which burned 5,005,872 acres of potential winter range for barren-ground caribou in north central Canada.

Figure 4–7. Erosion and fire. Subsurface erosion is coalescing to form a gully in the left foreground. The recently burned tufts of grasses can be readily seen. With the next rain this erosion will become even more severe. Fire, more than excessive animal use, is probably responsible.

This winter range lies largely within the *taiga,* and for caribou the greatest loss was the destruction of the very slow-growing arboreal lichens on which they feed. Moose *(Alces alces)* are favored by these fires, but the gain in moose fails to balance the loss of caribou (Scotter, 1971).

Natural fire on the eastern plains

In other areas fire is and has been a very important normal part of the environment. In the north central U.S.A., prairies extended eastward all the way to Ohio, forming a prairie peninsula. Madison, Wisconsin, lies within this former prairie land. Jutting westward from the east shore of Lake Mendota is a residential area called Maple Bluff. It still has many of the large, old, sugar maple trees *(Acer saccharum)* that were there when white men arrived. This wooded point was protected from the fires that swept in from the west during the spring. It was these fires that maintained the surrounding prairie in an area that had sufficient moisture to support a lush forest (Fig. 8–2). With the settlement of the area, the fires were stopped. Red *(Quercus rubra)* and black *(Quercus velutina)* oaks, which had existed as little bushes and were burned back about every 3 years, quickly formed forests, and a drastic change in animal life resulted. On some of the more droughty soils of the area, especially toward the western border of the state, there still remain scattered fire-resistant white *(Quercus alba)* and bur *(Quercus macrocarpa)* oaks with grassland beneath. Such *oak opening* country was formerly far more extensive. In the early 1940s, it was along a marshy edge of this area that I saw one of the last reported prairie chickens *(Tympanuchus cupido* and *T. pallidicinctus)* in southwestern Wisconsin, and it is the disappearance of such areas that has precipitated the disappearance of these animals.

Fires set by man

Similar to the oak opening country on the eastern edge of the great plains of North America are the tropical savannas of South America, Asia, and Africa. In Africa, the savanna supports, or at least did support, vast herds of grazing mammals and the predators that fed upon them, including man. Areas such as the African savannas and the North American oak opening country were rich in wildlife and were maintained by fire. Some of these fires were started by man, and even in North America this burning probably went on for perhaps 20,000–50,000 years. In Africa, where man evolved, he and his fires have probably been a feature of the environment for a million years or more. Although man and his fires are natural, with increases in the human population and the development of matches, the frequency with which fires are lit has increased immensely. If you have

Figure 4–8. This very extensive fire on the Nyika Plateau, Malawi, in 1969, was set to serve as a firebreak. On the ground, study has shown that burning on the plateau has been excessive. This was certainly an unnecessarily large firebreak. Accidental fires against which it was supposed to guard probably would not cause much more loss. See Fig. 4–9.

ever tried to make fire with a hand-twirled firestick as some Africans still do, you can readily appreciate the effect matches have had. Nowadays southern and central Africa are constantly shrouded in a pall of smoke as soon after the rainy season as it is possible to get the fires started. One can fly in a jet airliner for thousands of miles and never have a clear view of the ground because of the smoke (Fig. 4–8).

Just as the fires in the coast ranges of California (Fig. 2–7) are often lit by stock raisers hoping to improve grazing for their animals, so with the pastoralists in Africa (Fig. 4–9). Some think fire brings rain. Recent studies of air pollution and direct observation in Africa suggest that this is true, given the right climatological conditions. Unfortunately, while most of the African fires are burning, these climatological conditions are absent. In addition, fires in Africa are also lit to assist in hunting. Animals are driven into traps or are encircled with fire; the fire kills them, or maims them so that they are readily speared. Fire is also used in Africa to promote forestry in drier areas, and burning is done as soon as possible in the early part of the dry season. This removes combustible material from the forest, and

Figure 4–9. Fighting a grass fire encroaching on the Nyika Plateau, Malawi. These men are amazingly proficient at this. They prefer to use beaters constructed on the spot from green leafy branches rather than commercially made ones. A line of about eight men trot along the firefront, gauging their speed to the hotness of the fire. Each man, after the first, beats at the fire left by his predecessor. Trailing them at a distance of about 30–70 yards, two "clean-up" men beat out any flare-ups. These often result from smouldering zebra dung.

since most of the desired timber species are resistant to fire at this time of the year, they will be protected from the far hotter fires that occur later in the dry season. It is important to understand the ecological effects of these fires to realize how fire may be sensibly used by man.

Fire in african savannas

In general, in central and southern African savannas early fires cause an increase in woody species, which is often accompanied by severe soil erosion and *laterization,* especially in areas of deciduous scrub vegetation. Infrequent late fires which burn hotly just before the coming of the rains encourage the development of perennial grassland. Except for the timing of moisture and plant growth in different parts of the world, the general principles that control the effects of fire in African savannas probably apply elsewhere as well.

The perennial grasses of central Africa respond to the passage of fire by sending up succulent green blades. It is this "flushing" that the match-wielding pastoralist wishes his livestock to utilize. Wildlife also concentrate on recently burned areas to feed on the new green growth. The nutrients necessary for this growth are mobilized from the root reserves stored at the end of the previous growing season. Moisture is taken from the soil which is already extremely dry in most cases. If the grass can grow enough to replace the root reserves, no damage is done. In the case of early burns soon after the end of the rains, grazing must be severely limited if the grass is to grow enough to replace the root reserves. Also there must be considerable amounts of reserve water remaining in the soil. Without these two unusual circumstances, perennial grasses exhaust the soil water and then die back, having also depleted their root reserves. It is these reserves that normally give the grass a head start when the rains do come, allowing it to compete successfully with other plants.

In the drier savanna country of south central Africa, woody species lose their leaves early in the dry season. Most of the nonriparian (*riparian,* water edge) species are fire-hardy under these circumstances, and the relatively cool and slow fires at this time of the year do them no harm. Thus early burns leave woody species with a full capacity for growth as soon as the rains come again, and they compete very successfully with nutrient-depleted perennial grasses.

On the contrary, late fires just before the rains tend to have the opposite effect in this area. Most of the deciduous trees produce new leaves well before the first rains. If there is a good, dense mat of old grass below these trees to carry a fast, hot fire, such a late season fire will burn up into the branches of woody species and severely damage or even kill them. Thus the infrequent late-season fires caused by sparse populations of people using firesticks and by lightning strikes tend to maintain grassland and savannas by preventing succession to forests in southern, eastern, and central Africa.

Some fire–animal–climate interrelations

Why then are ecologists so worried about the loss of rich riparian woodlands in these areas? How did these woodlands manage to exist in former times? Two possible explanations have been suggested. One is that fires were so infrequent that forests were able to spread from riverbank areas, in a sense protecting themselves by sacrificing peripheral members which maintained such moist conditions that fires could not penetrate far. Another explanation has been partially documented by B. L. Mitchell (personal communication). He suggests that these and some upland wooded areas were protected against late-season hot fires by large grazing and browsing mammals which came into them to feed, rest, and avoid the great heat of the sun. By their feeding and trampling, these animals either removed or tramped down understory plants, ensuring that if a fire did succeed in penetrating the forest it would be a very slow and cool one which would not significantly harm the trees. Both factors probably operated, and were superimposed on the effects of local and widespread climatic variations.

We know that long-term climatic changes have occurred. What dismays those who have tried to encourage conservative land use in Africa is the constant blaming of the dry weather for erosion, grass depletion, highly irregular stream flows, and so on. Very frequently, excessive ill-timed burning and poor animal management are the real causes (Figs. 4–1 and 4–7). In some parts of any large continental area, such as North America or Africa, rainfall tends to be erratic in occurrence, amount, and distribution. This is especially true in more arid regions where the percentage difference in annual rainfall tends to be great (Trewartha, 1968). The biota is adjusted to these vagaries, and little serious damage occurs in the absence of mismanagement by man. However, as a result of effects of early burning during every dry season and of poor cattle management, each period of subnormal rainfall brings disastrous results. When the torrential rains characteristic of many such continental areas finally come, erosion is often severe.

Land management and fire

In the virgin groves of the coastal redwood forest, signs of former fires can be seen on the huge trunks. Their thick fibrous bark is highly fire-resistant; there are few substantial stands of coastal redwood that do not show the scars of former fires. It is hypothesized by some forest ecologists that fire is not only tolerated by redwoods but that it may be a necessary part of their environment (Becking, 1967). Many people are concerned that by the prevention of frequent small fires we have set the stage for huge devastating ones that will destroy rather than protect and assist natural forest processes.

They may be right. On a recent night in southern California, a 200,000-acre (80,970-hectare) fire had been contained. Another had been 80 percent contained after burning 8 million dollars worth of timber. One 35,000-acre blaze burning through chaparral started fires several miles away as a result of embers carried by 70-mile-per-hour winds. In all there were at least seven major fires recently controlled or burning partly out of control. And this did not include those elsewhere in the state. When the soil becomes saturated by the winter rains typical of this mediterranean climate, many steeper burned areas, unprotected by vegetation, will probably experience severe mud slides. For the large numbers of people living in chaparral areas, dry summers bring the threat of fire, and rainy winters the danger of slides.

We still have much to learn about the best conservation practices relative to fire ecology. Smokey the Bear is not the whole answer. Chaparral and fire, like redwoods and fire, seem to occur together. A change in our fire policies is obviously overdue. More fire research is needed, but we already know that African savannas are burned too frequently and many parts of North American wildlands too infrequently. We know that to support caribou we usually must exclude fire, and that we must do the same for deer on many of our more arid ranges. In coastal chaparral, however, fire is one of the most useful tools of land managers, along with intensive management of animals, for improving ranges for grazing and browsing mammals (Fig. 2–7).

SUGGESTED DISCUSSION MATERIAL

1. Investigate the private use of public lands in your state, province, or country. To what extent do private users determine the policies for their management? Do any abuses occur and, if so, how could they be halted or controlled? Is there a legal or traditional framework for determining the rights of citizens and others to use these lands in various ways? What consideration is given to nonconsumptive use, and do nonconsumptive users have a say in management of the public lands? Have use "rights" assumed a monetary value, so that they are bought and sold or otherwise bartered in private commercial channels? What are the sociological effects of public lands? Relate these to their history and to the social history of your area, and project the future needs for public lands. How could public lands be more closely integrated into the social and cultural realities of your area? Judge your conclusion from the standpoint of good conservation.

2. Can wilderness exist in a starving world?

3. What have been and are likely to be the social impacts of the so-called green revolution? Are there any dangers in genetic uniformity of food crops? Can you find case histories?

4. What are the attitudes of agriculturalists in your area toward conservation practices on the lands they manage? Examine their lands to determine how well conservation values are being maintained or enhanced. Relate attitudes to actions, and if there are discrepancies try to determine why they occur. Among other things, investigate tax structures, economic conditions, and peer pressure among agriculturalists. If changes should be made, what are they and how could they best be accomplished?

5. Select a moderate-sized portion of land known to you—perhaps a 100-square-mile piece—and develop a plan for its future. Consult with knowledgeable people. Relate your plan to prediction of population and technological changes in your region. Present your plans to your classmates for constructive criticism. Consider presenting an agreed-upon joint plan to a local body charged with land use planning. Were you able to find any study of land capability on which to base your plan? Could you obtain adequate maps and species lists? What reaction did you get from the body charged with land planning? Who actually determines land use in your area? What are the financial, social, and conservation implications of land use planning as it now exists in your region?

Weather Modification 5

We all modify microclimates by lighting campfires, by constructing houses, and so on. The ecological impacts of these actions are usually negligible when human populations are low and technology primitive. As populations and technology increase, so do ecological impacts. This results in greater and greater inadvertent effects on climate. Coupled with increases in these effects of human activities are conscious efforts to modify weather for man's benefit. But one man's benefit may be another's loss. Attempts at weather modification have been made to achieve both personal or general benefit and to harm others. It is very difficult to predict accurately the ecological effects of weather modification, because we know so little about the ecological and biological consequences climatic changes may produce, especially small, widespread changes of long duration. Thus there are good reasons for concern about both inadvertent and intentional weather modification. At the same time, the humanitarian aspects of weather modification should interest everyone.

EFFECTS OF CLOUD SEEDING

The first conclusively successful attempt to modify weather on a moderately extensive basis was made in 1946 by Irving Langmuir and Vincent Schaefer. They dropped Dry Ice pellets from an airplane into clouds over New England, and created a hole in the clouds. The supercooled water drops froze, fell, and evaporated lower down (Riehl, 1972). It soon became known that silver iodide smoke particles act as freezing nuclei at temperatures up to about −6°C (21°F), a higher temperature than that required for most natural freezing nuclei. If air is ascending, silver iodide smoke can be introduced from the ground, a cost advantage of this material. Silver iodide may also be introduced from aircraft, or fired into clouds with exploding artillery shells.

Given proper cloud conditions, the introduction of Dry Ice, silver iodide smoke, salt, or other nuclei can either cause or prevent precipitation. The introduction of a surplus of nuclei is termed *overseeding*. As a result of overseeding, the ice particles are too small to fall from the clouds, at least for a while. Thus cloud seeding can be used both to cause and to prevent precipitation.

Since fog is a cloud at ground level, it is not surprising that some kinds of fog can be cleared by seeding. Other types of fog such as *advection fog*, which occurs when warm, moisture-laden air blows across a cold surface, are very difficult to clear. Because of the effects of fog on aviation, considerable scientific effort is being put into fog clearance.

Hurricanes

There have been attempts to reduce and perhaps turn hurricanes by cloud seeding. *Hurricanes* are storms with winds of 75 miles per hour or faster. They cause severe loss of life and property. The November 1970 disaster along the Bangladesh coast at the head of the Bay of Bengal was an extreme example in which severe losses of life resulted partly from the crowding of excessive human population onto land especially vulnerable to hurricane devastation.

Hurricanes largely run on the energy released by condensation of water vapor. This vapor is usually supplied by warm ocean waters. By seeding clouds asymmetrically at a distance from a hurricane center, the pressure should be lowered on the outside and raised on the inside, thus reducing the pressure gradient and the wind speed. Likewise, there is some hope that the spreading of a thin, temporary, chemical film over the nearby ocean surface might reduce evaporation and so rob a potential hurricane of its energy source (Riehl, 1972). But tampering with hurricanes is hazardous for researchers, and potentially dangerous for those the storms may encounter. Few or none of each year's hurricanes can be experimented with in acceptable safety. Research results to date appear somewhat ambiguous. This is certainly not surprising when one considers the difficulties encountered in these studies, and the fact that considerable controversy still exists among weather modification specialists concerning the details of seeding more benign cloud formations.

Hail

Overseeding is used to prevent hail. In southern France one of the most intensive and extensive weather modification efforts is aimed at reducing agricultural losses from hail by cloud seeding with silver iodide smoke. Hail causes both agricultural and property losses. Probably the largest hailstone ever authenticated was picked up in Coffeyville, Kansas, on September 3, 1970. It weighed about 1 lb 11 oz (766 grams) and hit the earth at a speed of about 105 miles per hour (Roos, 1972). Although this is an extreme case, it is readily apparent that hailstones of half this size, or less, are capable of causing substantial damage. Even small ones with diameters of about 1 centimeter may damage agricultural crops.

Hail causes an estimated average annual crop loss of 284 million dollars in the U.S.A., based on 1968 price levels. Total property damage including crops amounts to about 315 million dollars. Crop hail losses are about 10 percent of all weather-related crop losses in the U.S.A., and this amounts to 10–15 percent of the annual national crop value. Thus in the U.S.A., national crop losses caused by weather amount to approximately 3.0 billion dollars each year (Changnon, 1972). From this we can readily appreciate why weather modification research receives financial support. In a world torn by hunger, we might anticipate even greater efforts to protect food production. Like most aspects of conservation, the combined exponential increase of population and technology rapidly decrease the time available for evaluating the potential impacts of weather modification.

SCHEMES FOR MAJOR CLIMATIC CHANGES

There have already been plans to institute major weather modifications. They have included proposals to deforest tropical South America, to melt the polar ice caps, and to change the circulation patterns of oceans. The impacts of such grandiose schemes on worldwide weather are doubtful, and we have almost no idea what the ecological and biological repercussions would be. To give a hint of the potential scope of the effects, it is only necessary to mention the recent findings of Namias (1972), which indicate that a devastating drought in northeastern Brazil resulted from an intense natural blocking of cyclonic movement in the Newfoundland–Greenland area.

Cyclones—not another name for tornados—have low-pressure centers around which air travels. Their winds are usually strong, and precipitation normally accompanies them. They are responsible for our most important day-to-day weather changes.

In the face of famine desperate efforts to increase food production by weather modification may occur. The risks involved will be enormous. It is important that such desperation with its potential deleterious effects be avoided by pursuing with utmost urgency the control of population and technology. In the meantime ill-conceived efforts to modify weather are bound to be proposed and carried out unless they are monitored closely. As Taubenfeld and Taubenfeld (1972) point out, "The [legal] cases suggest that in the short run it may be easier to stop weather modification through court injunctions than to collect damages afterward for injury, given the difficulty of proving cause and effect in weather changing. . . . Stress on potential harm to the environment may strengthen the preventive approach, since average effects over a period can be estimated even though it will remain difficult to prove the results of a specific act of weather modification."

POLLUTION AND THE CLIMATE OF URBAN AREAS

Movement of air pollutants in cities

The danger to human health from air pollution has stimulated intensive study of the weather in cities. Cities form heat islands which result in part from the great use of energy within them. This heat warms the air, and as it rises it carries pollutants upward. Ewig (1972) has calculated that for several of the largest cities in the U.S.A. in winter this urban heating is great enough to overcome the low-level, nighttime temperature inversions responsible for most severe pollution episodes. Observational data from many cities support his conclusions. He also calculates that by the mid-1990s New York City will avoid even the summertime nocturnal inversions caused by radiational cooling. This may perhaps seem too encouraging when one realizes that pollution has to go somewhere. Pollution has already been observed to follow vertical circular routes back into city centers, descending to join the cool air inflow that replaces the heated air flowing upward (Riehl, 1972). Such polluted air may also enter other pollution-producing areas and aggravate the problems there. Furthermore, midcity summer nights will be extremely warm. Much can be done to make city climates more livable. One improvement would be to reduce the summertime city core temperature if pollution is adequately controlled by other means.

The urban "cold doughnut"

A recent study (Outcalt, 1972) has identified a cool area, a "cold doughnut," which surrounds city centers and coincides with older residential areas and their many mature trees. As Outcalt (1972) notes, "This . . . appears to be the product of air flow over relatively wet and yet still rough surfaces." These surfaces are the mature trees. "This zone of the urban environment is critical as old residential areas which contain mature tree cover are prime targets for 'urban renewal'. . . . The beneficial effects of the tall tree annulus between the sparsely tree covered city core and tract subdivisions is often neglected in purely economic analyses." In fact, in his simulation studies he found in the urban "cold doughnut" lower midday temperatures than in any other area, even typical farmland. This "cold doughnut" area also showed the least diurnal temperature fluctuation. In terms of its temperature regime, it is the most livable area for humans.

Improving city climates

Other means to improve city climates are also possible. The long axis of a city could be planned to lie at right angles to the direction of the prevailing winds. Buildings could be aerodynamically designed to reduce obstructions to air movement. Green belts, especially with plenty of large trees, can ease both climatological and psychological distress. Most buildings in large cities are flat-topped, so the potential surface for plant growth is not greatly reduced. By growing plants on these buildings, irrigated by partly treated sewage, a useful contribution to climate, food, aesthetic, and sewage problems could be made. Industries could be restricted to the downwind side of a town, but better and quicker control of pollution would probably result if the city population received the full "benefit" of their effluent. The principle is the same as that involved in requiring water intakes to lie immediately downstream from outfalls.

EFFECTS OF POLLUTANTS
ON WORLD WEATHER

With industrialization has come the addition of many kinds of pollutants to the atmosphere. The increase in particulate matter should form nuclei for moisture condensation and increase precipitation downwind from major pollution sources. Data appear to show that this is happening, and if so it is one of man's most spectacular examples of weather modification (Riehl, 1972). The problem, of course, is to rule out the possibilities that other factors may be responsible.

Changes in albedo

On a much larger scale there is considerable concern that particulate matter and other pollution such as aircraft condensation trails are changing the earth's *albedo,* that is, its reflectance or degree of whiteness. This is measured as the ratio of light reflected to light received. If the albedo is being increased, this means that less solar energy is reaching the earth. To the extent that this is not compensated for by earth radiation trapped in the atmosphere and reflected or reradiated back to earth, the earth will cool.

The "greenhouse effect"

Correlated with these considerations are those of the effects of water vapor and carbon dioxide in the atmosphere. These two gases acting together cause the greenhouse effect. They accomplish this because they have a physical property similar to that of ordinary glass; that is, they are transparent to the short wavelengths of visible light and are also effective absorbers and reradiators of longer-wave heat radiation. With carbon dioxide and water vapor in the air above the earth, radiant energy is in a sense trapped, as it is in a greenhouse. But the trapping is not complete because water vapor is transparent not only to visible light but also to heat rays of wavelengths near 10 microns, the so-called window. This effect has substantial climatic implications, because the strongest longwave earth radiation is normally of about this wavelength.

World temperature changes

From roughly 1850 to 1950, the earth's temperature has risen about 1°F (0.56°C), the greatest rise occurring at higher latitudes. During this same period the concentration of atmospheric carbon dioxide has risen by at least 10 percent (Riehl, 1972). Since 1950 however, world temperatures seem to have declined, but atmospheric carbon dioxide concentrations have not decreased. Atmospheric pollution may have increased the albedo sufficiently to counteract the greenhouse effect of increased atmospheric carbon dioxide. At the moment these explanations are somewhat speculative, but their real possibility points to both the need for research and the need for caution in causing additional increases in atmospheric pollution.

Admittedly, a 1°F change in world temperature sounds unimportant, yet Riehl (1972) says, "If true, it is the *major weather modification* accomplished by man." He comments further, "If the polar ice sheets were to expand or shrink a little, substantial changes in the heat budget of the polar zones would follow as the size of the high-albedo area changed." Snow, like thick clouds and heavy smog, has a high albedo and thus reduces the absorption of solar energy by the earth's surface.

Any substantial change in albedo, hence in earth temperature could possibly have massive effects. The reason is that albedo changes probably set up temporary, positive feedback loops; an increase in albedo causes cooling, more snow, and therefore a further albedo increase. The opposite is probably also true, but there is little likelihood that we could dangerously reduce the albedo. What we must especially guard against is a major inadvertent increase in albedo.

We are now probably capable of producing extensive intentional weather modifications, but we have no way to predict the consequences accurately and in detail. Worldwide social pressures may stimulate drastic efforts to modify weather. If these efforts are carried out irresponsibly, the consequences could be catastrophic. However, intelligent local manipulation of weather might go far in improving man's existence, while creating only minor disadvantages.

SUGGESTED DISCUSSION MATERIAL

1. How do living organisms create microclimates?

2. What could be done by a country to wage undeclared war on another through weather modification?

3. What are the actual physical principles involved in the formation of rain, snow, and hail? What happens in clouds that result in these occurring.

4. Which direction do prevailing winds blow in your area and why? What ecological impact does this have on vegetation and animal life? What relation does it have to pollution and to the use of natural resources in your area?

5. Look into the recent literature on oceanography, meteorology, and geology, and, based on this information, explore the possible implications of major weather modifications.

6. Explore the architectural, economic, and social implications of constructing cities to achieve optimum climatic and social conditions for their residents. Do not neglect the problems your city may cause for those residing beyond its borders.

7. Explore in depth the greenhouse effect. What are the implications for energy conservation? How can these principles be applied to housing? Would it be possible or practical to reduce significantly the output of carbon dioxide, and if so, how?

8. Do you have an organization that monitors weather modifications in your area? Is weather modification being practiced there? What is the extent of general awareness and what are the general feelings concerning this modification?

9. Explore the literature concerning other aspects of weather such as tornados, anticyclones, adiabatic cooling and warming, squall lines,

variations in wind speed with height above the ground, cold air drainage, and so on. What ecological effects do they have?

10. What could be done inexpensively to improve the local climate in the area where you now live? For example, trees could be planted to create a windbreak. Do you have air pollution? Have you looked at your home area in the early morning just before sunrise after a night with little or no wind? If not, do so. You may have more air pollution than you realize. What can you do about it?

Wildlife   6

SPORT VERSUS COMMERCIAL UTILIZATION
—THE MANAGEMENT OF WILDLIFE

Historical background

The hunting of game for sport was practiced well before the twelfth century in central Europe. (Remember that the invention of gunpowder occurred about 1300 and that Columbus discovered America in 1492, nearly two centuries later.) After a hunt was over in Europe, the animals killed were utilized. Nowadays, such animals and animal parts not kept by a hunter are sold, and the proceeds used to help defray the cost of maintaining wildlife and wildlife habitats.

The first European settlers in North America apparently started out with the idea that the natural resources of the New World were inexhaustible. Most of them were common people who had been able to hunt in Europe only by poaching game that legally belonged to the aristocracy. Their attitudes were probably influenced by the landowners' use of huge ferociously toothed steel man traps and gin traps to capture them. The British bred huge mastiffs and more agile, somewhat smaller but equally dangerous bull mastiff dogs for the express purpose of attacking poachers. There is little doubt that these dogs were trained in such a way that they sometimes killed people (Grosvenor and Severy, 1958).

With this background it was natural that in North America people considered game as belonging to everybody; so in the U.S.A. wildlife is legally held in trust for the people by the state. It was also natural that European settlers continued to sell game, since this had been done in Britain and elsewhere by poachers as well as landowners. This combination of attitudes, as reasonable as they seemed at the time, set the stage for the extermination of the passenger pigeon *(Ectopistes migratorius),* and the near extermination of the bison *(Bison bison),* and the common egret *(Casmerodius albus),* to name but three.

European settlers considered the New World a public area. (American Indians believed that they and *not* the Europeans owned the right to use it.) Whenever a public resource is opened to private economic exploitation, the forces of extinction are unleashed. North America was settled by people who energetically sought to increase their wealth, and in so doing they exterminated the Carolina parakeet *(Conuropsis carolinensis),* the great auk *(Pinguinus impennis),* the passenger pigeon, the heath hen *(Tympanuchus cupido cupido),* the sea mink *(Mustela macrodon),* and so on. They need not have done so.

Finally, exploitation became so blatant that only a vulture could have looked on the carnage with favor; bison were shot by the thousands for their tongues, deer killed for their skins, and egrets shot from their nests for their nuptial plumes. Finally, some of our forefathers decided to stop some of the slaughter. So we still can see bison, but never the dark herds moving before the March winds under skeins of geese, swans, and cranes.

Not only are we aesthetically impoverished, but it is probable that through careful management of these wild animals we could be as well fed as with the introduced animals that have replaced them. No one can refute this, because efforts to learn to manage wildlife as a food source are almost nonexistent compared with those that have been expended on domestic animals. It would probably take a generation at least to return to management of wildlife as a principal food source in North America, even after being proved beyond virtually all doubt to be preferable to the nearly exclusive use of domestic livestock. Thus our forefathers have removed one of our options.

The legal result of all the carnage in North America was the establishment of laws to protect wildlife, and to make certain that they were obeyed people were hired to enforce them. These laws protected some animals completely, left others completely unprotected or even encouraged their extermination, and dealt with others in various intermediate ways. Efforts were made to stop the commercial use of many species.

Use of public resources for private gain

Commercial use was the enemy, but we have failed to recognize that *private* commercial use of a *public* resource is by far the most dangerous. Commercial use of a resource by its private owner is less dangerous and may insure its continued abundance. In the U.S.A., an example is domestic livestock, and in Europe, wildlife species hunted for sport such as red deer *(Cervus elaphus),* roe deer *(Capreolus capreolus),* wild boar *(Sus scrofa),* and capercailzie *(Tetrao urogallus).* It is this principle that conserves game in some parts of Africa through commercial game ranching and safari hunting. Many cattle ranching enterprises in Africa are now also involved in game ranching. Zebra *(Equus burchelli)* that formerly were shot on sight because they eat grass and sometimes break cattle fences are now carefully conserved, because they are worth about as much per head as cows and cost far less to produce (Fig. 6–1).

Failure to recognize that it is the private exploitation of a public resource that sets the stage for extermination also leads to the passage of poor laws. The California legislature has had before it a law forbidding the importation of animals or their parts if they are considered endangered. The ultimate aim of the law is good, to prevent their extermination. Unfortunately, any blanket prohibition will do harm as well as good. Among species listed as endangered is the leopard *(Panthera pardus).* At the moment leopard skins are so valuable that some private game ranchers look on them as one of the animals to be cropped for profit on a sustained basis. If they become unsalable, they will be regarded by their private

Figure 6–1. Zebra family in Wankie National Park, Rhodesia. These beautiful animals are now being conserved on private game ranches because of their commercial value. Formerly, people were hired to exterminate them on some of these same ranches.

"owners" as killers of animals that are salable and also as hazards to human life. Such animals are killed by all methods, fair or foul. A slight change in the wording of such a bill would make an important difference, allowing the sale of leopard skins from properly husbanded populations while cracking down hard on exploiters. Futhermore, by improving the market for properly husbanded leopards, it could well induce others to start proper management (see page 112).[1]

Utilization for conservation

Private ownership does not guarantee proper husbandry. For this reason we have laws governing our treatment of animals, and *badly need* others to govern our treatment of the environment. To prevent overexploitation of privately owned wildlife in West Germany today, strict laws control its utilization. But at least under private ownership we avoid the near guarantee of overexploitation of a public resource taken for profit by private individuals. This protection is also achieved in the U.S.S.R., where wildlife is owned by the state. There the saiga antelope *(Saiga tatarica)* serves as an example of what can be done to preserve and at the same time utilize a wildlife species. "During the past three decades the saiga has become the most widespread of the wild ungulates in the U.S.S.R. Prior to this it was so rare as to be on the verge of extinction. . . . At the present time hunters bag 250,000–300,000 saigas annually. . . . The saiga best illustrates the efficiency of nature preservation measures in bringing about economic advantages" (Bannikov et al., 1967).

Sport hunting versus trapping regulations

In the U.S.A. fur bearers are legally distinguished from game mammals. They may include muskrat *(Ondatra zibethica)*, beaver *(Castor canadensis)*, mink *(Mustela vison)*, river otter *(Lutra canadensis)*, opossum *(Didelphis marsupialis)*, striped skunk *(Mephitis mephitis)*, badger *(Taxidea taxus)*, Arctic ground squirrel *(Citellus undulatus)*, and so on. Fur bearers taken under a trapping license may be sold. A trapping license often permits other methods of capturing fur bearers, such as shooting or snaring. Hunting licenses usually allow capture only by shooting with specific firearms and ammunition or with bows and arrows.

In Wisconsin black bears [*Ursus (Euarctos) americanus*] have been covered under both sport hunting and trapping regulations. During the

---

[1]A recent addition to Section 6530 of the Penal Code of California forbids the sale of parts such as meat or skins of several species. Among these is the zebra. Let us hope this is not the start of a return to zebra extermination in southern Africa.

sport hunting season no part of a bear taken could be sold, but during the trapping season any part could be sold.

Deer are covered under sport hunting regulations. It is illegal to sell their meat, but in most states one may sell the skin, antlers, hooves, or tails.

Thus in Wisconsin bears are at times sport animals and at times commercial animals, while deer in California are sport animals on the inside and commercial animals on the outside and at the extremities. Fur bearers are used commercially. With such apparent inconsistencies, it is difficult to see why there is such a strong feeling against utilization of wildlife for profit. Perhaps it results partly from our heritage of free hunting on public land and partly from a fear of overexploitation for commercial gain. The latter results from a general failure to understand that it was private commercial exploitation of public wildlife that caused havoc here. Private exploitation of publicly owned fisheries is likewise severely endangering them in the world today. The disgraceful overexploitation of whales is a good but very unfortunate example (Ehrenfeld, 1970; Hickel, 1971).

Sport hunting is now sold in the U.S.A., but in most states it is done in a peculiar manner to stay within the law. Instead of selling animals, a landholder sells the right of entrance. He can sell this right to as many people as pay his price. The abundance and quality of game and hunting opportunities are related to the number of hunters, the size of their bags, and the season lengths; but because of state game regulations based on public ownership of wildlife, proper management is usually impossible. This is especially true of big game.

Doe hunts

In California during the 1970 regular season, only adult male deer could be taken, as had been the case for a great many years. In managing for maximum production of meat in a *polygynous* mammal (one in which a male mates with more than one female), it is essential that after optimum stocking is reached surplus females be removed. This is not permitted in California, and as a result the deer, vegetation, land, hunters, landowners, and sightseers all suffer (Fig. 4–2). Perhaps the real reasons behind the doe hunt battles would surprise many an unsuspecting sportsman. Good deer management and associated land use practices probably are the last and least considerations of those who oppose removal of surplus females. Land damage by excessive populations of any species removes options for the use of that land.

Good wildlife management in the U.S.A. is not possible, because few if any game management agencies have the resources, inclination, or perhaps even the right to provide the intensive assistance necessary for optimum private management. In parts of Texas this may not be true (Teer,

Thomas, and Walker, 1965). There, permits to shoot deer are sold, rather than the right of entrance, and these permits are for female as well as for male deer. The permits are provided by the game department. This way of handling deer hunting is possible because of the unique legal status of wildlife in that state. But even in Texas management is unsatisfactory (Teer, Thomas, and Walker, 1965). The largely rule-of-thumb management of private big game on the shooting grounds of Europe is probably superior in practice. The King Ranch of Texas is probably a notable exception, employing several competent wildlife biologists.

Game management in Europe

European game management schemes are superior in four ways. First, full-time gamekeepers are employed. These men live much of their lives out-of-doors with the animals, and make a real effort to know and record the numbers of each sex and age group. These gamekeepers also remove surplus animals not taken by sport hunters, and carry out other intensive management such as planting food plots and constructing shooting blinds. Second, all trophies and kill records, at least in West Germany, are submitted for study to public officials who also evaluate the proposed management and harvest for the following year. This group then either approves a landowner's or hunting group's proposal or insists on certain changes. Third, sportsmen have a strong feeling of personal possession and responsibility for the animals on the lands over which they have the right to hunt. Because of this feeling, associated traditions, prestige, and the necessity for passing examinations before receiving a hunting license, they probably have far more knowledge of the animals and the lands on which they hunt than does the average North American sportsman. Fourth, harvested wildlife is sold, and the proceeds help pay for wildlife management. This direct tangible return fosters good management.

Some changes needed and the reasons

If we in the U.S.A. are ever to achieve intensive management of our big game herds, we must somehow foster a change in both the attitudes we have toward wildlife and the legal framework within which wildlife management must be carried out. Private landowners cannot be given complete freedom to do with their wildlife as they choose, because a significant number are sure to abuse this freedom. But they must be given far more incentive to manage wildlife properly than they have at present.

Consumptive exploitation of a public resource for private gain leads toward extinction of the resource, as has been pointed out. The corollaries are worth remembering. Utilization of a private resource for private gain

can, if properly controlled, ensure survival of the resource, as can utilization of a public resource by a public agency working for public benefit. The
highly successful management of North Pacific fur seals *(Callorhinus ur-
sinus)* by the U.S. government is an example of the latter. In this instance
the people of four countries (Japan, the U.S.S.R., Canada, and the U.S.A.)
have benefited, and the fur seal has been returned to abundance from the
brink of extinction (Maxwell, 1967). A similar and also successful effort has
been applied to the saiga antelope in the U.S.S.R. (Bannikov et al., 1967)
(see page 102).

ENDANGERED SPECIES

Need to preserve genetic information

Endangered species concern us for several reasons. One of these is that
the information recorded in their genes may prove to be of great value in
the future should environmental or social conditions change, or should we
obtain new insight into old dilemmas. In an effort to conserve such diversity of genetic materials, a museum of living fungal strains is maintained at
California State University, Humboldt; and a somewhat similar bank of
genetic strains of crop plants is located at The National Seed Storage
Laboratory, U.S.D.A., Fort Collins, Colorado. These efforts and similar
ones are examples of what can and should be done for other groups of
organisms.

Purely by accident, most of the genes of the lions that formerly lived
in the Barbary region of North Africa have probably been preserved in the
zoo lions of the world, even though the Barbary lion has been extinct in
the wild for many years (Guggisberg, 1963).

Another similar example is the maintenance of the unique Père David's deer *(Cervus davidianus)* in the Imperial Hunting Park of the Chinese
emperor south of Peking. No others existed in 1865 when Père David
obtained from the emperor's park the first specimen known to the western
world. Apparently, these deer had ceased to exist in the wild as long ago
as the Shang Dynasty (1766–1122 B.C.), and had survived for 2000 years
in parks. In 1894 a flood of the Hun Ho River breached the walls of the
Imperial Hunting Park. The deer that escaped were eaten by the famine-
stricken peasants. During the Boxer Rising in 1900 international troops
destroyed all the animals that remained in the park except a few that were
taken to Peking. By 1920 all of these had also perished. Fortunately, some
time earlier other breeding groups of these deer had been established in
Europe. The Duke of Bedford acquired 16 animals from European zoos in
1900 and 1901. These formed the nucleus of a breeding herd at Woburn
Abbey. After World War II animals were distributed to various zoos, so the

species still survives in the zoological gardens of the world (Simon, 1966).

In the Bialowieza Forest in Poland lived the last herd of wisent or European bison *(Bison bonasus)*, which are very close relatives of the American bison *(Bison bison)*. Crosses of the pure stock with American bison have been made in an attempt to conserve genetic information in the hybrids. The last wild herd (737 head in 1914) living in the Bialowieza Forest was destroyed in World War I. Later, animals were purchased from several sources of captive animals, and in 1956 wisent were again released into the Bialowieza Forest. By 1966 the herd numbered 57, of which 34 had been born in the wild. In 1965 the world population was 267 animals (Simon, 1966). This animal, standing 6 feet or more at the shoulder, is not only a potential meat animal, but also a most impressive aesthetic asset.

Aesthetic values

The whooping crane *(Grus americana)*, the ivory-billed woodpecker *(Campephilus principalis)*, the Mexican grizzly *(Ursus horribilis)*, the snow leopard *(Uncia uncia)*, and the Siberian tiger *(Panthera tigris)* are all animals whose aesthetic value is easily appreciated. All are endangered. If you have ever seen a good zoo example of a magnificent, huge, long-haired Siberian tiger, you can certainly imagine the thrill of seeing one stalking through the snow among the birches of Siberia. Such vicarious aesthetic appreciation is one of the real assets provided by wild animals and wild places.

Unpredictable future utility

Another reason why we need to prevent the extermination of species is that we are completely unable to predict their future utility for mankind. In the fourteenth century, the Black Death, partly caused by bubonic plague, swept through Europe several times, killing an estimated one-quarter of the total human population. Again in 1665 over 68,000 people died of plague in London (Encyclopedia Brittanica, 1946). The common Norway rat *(Rattus norvegicus)* and the roof rat *(Rattus rattus)* carried the fleas that transmitted the disease to man.

At present, a somewhat similar problem is being confronted in Africa where tsetse flies *(Glossina* spp.) not only transmit trypanosomes from wildlife to man and his domestic animals, but also serve as hosts for the multiplication of the parasites. A massive effort is being mounted to exterminate tsetse flies, five species in all. The hope is that this in turn will exterminate the trypanosomes. What would have happened if the same approach had been applied with success to the Norway rat in the fourteenth century? Certainly, it would have meant that at the very least some other mammal would have had to replace the domesticated Norway rat as one of the most important scientific laboratory animals. There is hardly any aspect of the physical or mental health of humans that has not been studied to our benefit in some way or other through the use of the laboratory rat.

As objectionable as tsetse flies are, can we really afford to exterminate them? There is little doubt that tsetse flies are in a sense endangered in spite of their present dangerous abundance. But their extermination is surely not necessary, and because it eliminates all possible choices associated with them it is probably not a wise move to make.

There is still another reason why we should be concerned about endangered species. It is that perhaps what endangers them may eventually endanger us. By studying them, we may learn in time to protect ourselves.

Taxonomy and amount of concern

The International Union for Conservation of Nature and Natural Resources publishes and updates the *Red Data Books* which list endangered species of mammals, birds, amphibians and reptiles, and angiosperm plants (Simon, 1966; Vincent, 1966; Honegger, 1968; Melville, 1970). Upon reading these lists, or the *Red Book on Rare and Endangered Fish and Wildlife of the United States* issued by the U.S. Bureau of Sport Fisheries and Wildlife, one can immediately see that some of the endangered animals are subspecies. Other subspecies may exist in very abundant and healthy localized populations.

At what taxonomic level should we become concerned with possible extinctions? How concerned should we be? After all, no two individuals are identical unless derived from the same zygote (fertilized egg) or from a single parent, as in vegetatively reproducing forms or parthenogenetic forms (organisms producing eggs that develop without fertilization).[2] Each individual carries genetic information possibly also carried by others, but not in the same unique arrangement. As we compare individuals that differ from each other at the subspecific, specific, and generic levels, the genetic information they carry in common becomes less and less the farther apart they are on the phylogenetic scale.

From this point of view, it would be a greater disaster to lose the pronghorn antelope *(Antilocapra americana)* than the polar bear [*Ursus*

---

[2]Parthenogenesis has been defined facetiously as "procreation without recreation." "In nature," it occurs only rarely in advanced forms (for example, turkeys), but it is the normal mode of reproduction in many insects and plants. It has been experimentally induced in frogs, silkworms, and rabbits.

(Thalarctos) maritimus]. The reason is that the pronghorn is the only species of the only genus in its phylogenetic family still in existence. In contrast, the genus *Ursus* includes several species in addition to the polar bear. Nonetheless the polar bear fills such a unique niche that our argument may appear pointless. Not so. It is at the specific and subspecific levels that decisions will be made. It seems to make good sense to be more concerned with the loss of a species than with the loss of a subspecies. But even the loss of a subspecies is to be avoided if at all possible. In other words, it is the amount of genetic redundancy that should determine the extent of our concern for endangered organisms. Subspecies comprising a species are expected to have more genetic information in common than are species comprising a genus. Thus the amount of genetic redundancy is in general greater among subspecies within a species than among species within a genus, and so on. As we consider organisms related at specific, generic, and higher phylogenetic levels, that is, organisms more and more distantly related, the amount of genetic redundancy becomes less and less. The more distantly two organisms are related, the less genetic information they share. Thus we should normally be more concerned with the loss of an animal such as the mountain beaver *(Aplodontia rufa)*, the sole member of a peculiar and unique terrestrial rodent family, than we should with the loss of a subspecies of the California meadow mouse *(Microtus californicus)*. The California meadow mouse is one of many species in the very widespread and successful subfamily Microtinae.

Distribution and amount of concern

The question of the loss of subspecies or geographically distinct races is intimately related to the distribution of animals. In parts of its range, a species may be in great danger of extinction, while elsewhere it lives in healthy abundance with little danger that this condition will change much in the near future. An example is the nyala *(Tragelaphus angasi)* in Malawi and Rhodesia, where it is certainly not secure. On the contrary, in South Africa it is excessively abundant in some localities. This large, beautiful antelope occurs in Malawi in dense lowland thickets which grow on rich, black soils which can support intensive agriculture. With a very dense and rapidly increasing human population, the pressure for human occupancy of these lands is great. A country too poor to preserve natural aesthetic assets such as the nyala and the lowland thickets teeming with life is a sad place. Hopefully, Malawi will avoid such poverty. The nyala will serve as one barometer of Malawi's success. Although it will be unfortunate to lose this animal from Malawi, the implications of this loss in terms of human living conditions are more important than the loss of the antelope.

Accelerating rate of extinctions

In geological perspective few if any species have avoided evolutionary change, and the earth itself has also undergone considerable geological evolution during the time that living forms have existed. There is no denying that species arose and became extinct long before the first protohominid appeared, unless of course one chooses to believe that the entire fossil record was created *in situ*. Thus one cannot deny that extinction is normal in geological perspective. This is, however, a far cry from agreeing that extinction *at present rates* is normal in geological perspective. "The pace of these exterminations has accelerated greatly and most exterminations have occurred in recent years. The rate of exterminations has increased fifty-fivefold in the past century and a half and over 50% of the total known losses have occurred since 1900, in less than 4% of the 2000 years of record" (Talbot, 1970).

It is verbal trickery to claim, as many have, that since the fossil record shows so many examples of the extinction of species we should not worry about the extinction of species that is occurring nowadays. When you read or hear such an argument, it pays to consider what the speaker may gain for himself by espousing such a notion.

The rate of extinction has certainly accelerated with the advent of technological man. Although this can be established with little doubt for the period since written records have been kept, it is not easy to do so for earlier periods. Nonetheless, there is growing evidence that extinction at the hands of man greatly predated the invention of writing (Guthrie, 1972; Martin, 1970).

Pleistocene extinctions

The Pleistocene extinctions did not occur at the same time in all parts of the world. But they apparently followed fairly closely the arrival of man or his obvious increase in abundance (Martin, 1970).[3] Not only that, these extinctions were almost entirely limited to larger mammals. Prolific, small, secretive mammals evidently did not succumb at a similar rate. The same appears to be true of birds and reptiles, and there were no increases in the extinction of amphibians or fish. From the archeological record, it has been well established that men of Pleistocene times hunted the great animals now extinct. For example, you can view the skeleton of a huge mammoth (*Mammuthus* sp.) in the Denver Museum in Colorado and see the beauti-

---

[3] The most popular alternate explanation of the Pleistocene extinctions is that they were caused by climatic changes.

fully made chipped-stone projectile point found embedded in one of its bones.

Several hypothetical explanations as to how man may have accomplished these extinctions have been presented (Krantz, 1970). Many forms may have been exterminated directly by hunting. The extinction of powerful predators such as saber-tooth cats *(Smilodon spp.)*, dire wolves *(Canis dirus)*, and short-faced bears *(Arctodus sp.)* has been attributed to both direct attack by man and to unsuccessful competition with man for the same food resources. Pack-hunting man with his fire, spears, throwing boards, darts, traps, and superior intelligence probably reduced prey populations and finally exterminated them along with the great carnivores that were dependent upon their natural increase.

Attributes of an exterminator

Man, being omnivorous, can support himself on vegetable matter, insects, crustaceans, molluscs, bird eggs, lizards, and so on. In addition, archeological evidence and the study of the few remaining simple cultures show that man was and is a very capable and eager hunter. No other omnivores hunt large game in well-coordinated packs, and no carnivore or omnivore comes close to having the intelligence and adaptability of man.

Thus man has all the attributes of an exterminator. He can maintain substantial populations by scavenging, digging roots, and eating fruits, leaves, grains, and so on. At the same time, he has both the ability and the desire to hunt large animals. Since the size of his population, unlike that of saber-tooth cats and dire wolves, is not necessarily determined by the amount of meat he can obtain, he has the ability at least locally to hunt to extinction any species lacking excellent defenses against him and/or the ability to reproduce at a high rate.

Man also has used fire to pursue game. One can only infer that fire was used in the past for hunting, as it is today. Ring fires kill and wound the animals caught within, making the injured survivors more vulnerable to spearmen. In the modern day *chilas* (annual ritualistic group hunts) that take place on the flats of the Kafue River in Zambia, fire is used to drive both lechwe *(Kobus leche)* and the very dangerous African buffalo *(Syncerus caffer)* to waiting hunters. Wildlife is attracted to new growth following fires, and some burning surely was (and is) designed to attract animals to places where they can easily be located and successfully hunted.

Endangering by human-induced environmental changes

Man-caused fires have been important in shaping the vegetation in much of the world (see page 80). In the U.S.A. the long grass prairie and the prairie–deciduous forest ecotone area, where the two intergrade, were maintained by fires that were swept eastward by the strong west winds of spring. Likewise, the vast savanna lands of east and central Africa are also maintained by fire. Both the lack of fire and too frequent and ill-timed fires encourage the growth of woody species or, in some areas, unpalatable, fire-resistant grasses. These kinds of vegetational changes may have been important in the extinction of some of the Pleistocene megafauna.

Whether they were or not, there is little doubt that now the principal threats to species in developed countries are the changes wrought by man's technology. Sterilization or partial sterilization of carnivores at the apex of the food pyramid (through ingestion of certain biologically concentrated insecticides such as DDT), cutting of virgin forests, aforestation of former grasslands and savannas, prevention of fire, excessive use of fire, settlement of valley lands, elimination of wildlife winter ranges, irrigation of lands near water thus limiting the dry-season range of wildlife, paving of vast areas for roads, replacement of native fauna by domestic stock, draining of marshes or their conversion to rice culture, filling of estuaries, and so on all contribute to the accelerating decrease in numbers and kinds of wild organisms. And behind it all lurks an unbridled increase in human numbers.

Some things to do and not to do

Unfortunately, we would lose too many species if we were to concentrate our entire effort toward halting the human population explosion. To protect other species as well as ourselves, we need to reduce our consumption of resources and channel our necessary consumption so as to create the least environmental mischief. Many additional things can and are being done to protect endangered species. These include the setting up of sanctuaries such as that for the California condor (Gymnogyps californianus), prohibition of the killing of endangered species, embargoes on the use of endangered species or their parts as items of trade, and so on.

Any of these actions could sooner or later do harm to a species, as well as help secure its continued existence. To explain: We tend to sit back and congratulate ourselves when we have achieved some measure of protection for a species. While we are busy patting our own backs—and ignoring the species concerned—it may well be suffering more than it did before protection. Therefore it is important to keep constant watch on endangered species even after they have been given protection. Only in this way can new threats to their existence be detected and countered in time.

Sometimes well-meaning efforts to protect species may have exactly the opposite effect. A recent amendment of the Penal Code of the State of California is probably a case in point. Amendment SB1614 to Section 6530 added zebras and other species to the list of dead animals or animal parts that may not be sold in California. If this embargo becomes widespread, zebras in southern Africa will again become endangered. The reason is straightforward. Zebras sometimes compete with cattle for forage, and they occasionally break fences. If zebra hides become much reduced in value, the zebra's only substantial and direct economic value remaining would be its meat. On this basis zebra probably could not compete successfully with cattle, given the prejudices that ranchers in Africa harbor against them.

Prior to the beginning of game ranching in Rhodesia, hunters were hired to exterminate zebra on large private ranches. One farmer bragged to us that he had managed to fence off all water on his ranch. Between his shooting of the weakened animals struggling against the fences and the mortality from lack of water, he felt that he was finally going to be rid of them. Zebra hides now make them approximately equal in value to range cattle. As a result, most farmers have completely changed their attitudes and have been carefully husbanding their zebra. Widespread laws patterned after the recent amendment to the Penal Code of California will surely bring a return of the most cruel and efficient efforts to exterminate them.

Such a mentality is not limited to certain kinds of people or to certain areas. A rancher in northern California owns extensive property which supports a very large herd of black-tailed deer (Odocoileus hemionus). Some invade his home garden plot and eat the plants. Simple fences have failed to keep them out. Since he considers it too much trouble to build an adequate fence or to obtain a permit to shoot the deer and to see that the meat is properly utilized or sent to charity, he has devised a far simpler way of protecting his garden. His young children shoot the animals in the paunch with a .22-caliber rifle. According to the rancher, this has solved his problem; shot this way, the deer run off into the woods to die. Besides, the children could not be convicted even if they were caught. Would he do likewise to his cattle or domestic sheep? Potentially each of the deer is as valuable as a domestic sheep, but in his impoverished mind, they lack even sufficient aesthetic value to save them. His children will probably perpetuate his attitudes.

For such people, an economic gain they can personally realize is all that will induce them to give protection to a species. Thus to ensure that we will not endanger species, it would be useful to assign to them publicly recognized aesthetic, scientific, and economic values. Public recognition that we cannot predict the potential value a species may eventually have for us will help in its conservation. Also helpful will be general public realization that to ensure our future we must leave open as many possible choices as we can. Extinction of a species eliminates all possibilities related to its existence.

INTRODUCTIONS AND REINTRODUCTIONS OF ORGANISMS

Regaining biotic diversity

Biotic diversity tends to favor the stability of biotic communities; that is, the more diverse a community, the more stable it tends to be (page 35). In a time of biological extinctions resulting both directly and indirectly from man's activities, should we protect existing diversity by preventing further extinctions? It certainly seems prudent to do so. If this point of view is accepted, should we not then seek to regain lost diversity through the reintroduction of locally exterminated species? This also, as a general rule, seems logical.

Now we must ask ourselves two further questions. If the previously existing local race of the species we wish to reintroduce can no longer be obtained, are we justified in using another race or perhaps another closely allied species? The second question concerns the amount of time since the species or genus became locally exterminated. For example, there have been few objections to the reintroduction in October 1971 of the desert subspecies of the bighorn sheep *(Ovis canadensis)* into Lava Beds National Monument along the northern border of California. These sheep became extinct in that area about 50 years ago (Buechner, 1960). Would we be willing to reintroduce a species that became locally extinct 200 years ago, 400 years ago, or 4000 years ago?

Four thousand years represents about one-third of the time that has passed since many large mammals became extinct in North America (Martin and Wright, 1967) (see page 109). In North America during the Pleistocene extinctions, 35 large mammalian genera listed in Table 6–1 became extinct (Martin, 1970). Would we be justified in reintroducing animals extinct in North America that still survive elsewhere, such as the saiga antelope? Would we be justified in introducing close relatives of extinct forms, such as modern camels (*Camelus* spp.)? Some people, I suppose, would object to the introduction of Siberian tigers to replace saber-tooth cats or to the introduction of African elephants to replace mammoths or mastodons (*Mammut* spp.). Such possibilities illustrate that the problems of introductions and reintroductions of species are matters of degree and not of kind.

Human attitudes

Some introductions have certainly been unfortunate. The chestnut blight introduced from Europe to North America has nearly eliminated the American chestnut *(Castenea dentata),* a tree much appreciated by humans as well as by squirrels. The small Indian mongoose *(Herpestes auropunctatus)* introduced into Hawaii is credited with the elimination on several islands of certain small, colonial, ground-nesting birds such as the Hawaiian dark-rumped petrel *(Pterodroma phaeopygia)* (Hinton and Dunn, 1967). Both in Hawaii and Jamaica some still consider this mongoose an asset because of its predation on rats in sugarcane fields.

Other cases are less clear. The introduction of the European rabbit *(Oryctolagus cuniculus)* into Australia is a prime example, because it is usually cited as the perfect illustration of an ill-conceived introduction. These animals compete for forage with domestic sheep *(Ovis aries),* also introduced. Human opinion in Australia and many other places favors

Table 6–1. Pleistocene megafauna of North America (Irvingtonian and Blancan extinction omitted)*

Order or class	Rancholabrean extinction in North America (last 15,000 yrs)	Surviving in North America
Edentata ground sloths, armored edentates, giant armadillo	7 genera	none
Carnivora bears, saber-tooth cats, living "cats" and "dogs"	4 genera†	5 (4) genera‡
Proboscidea elephants	3 genera	none
Artiodactyla cloven-hoofed ungulates including pigs, camels, pronghorns, deer, muskoxen, bovids, and others	15 genera†	9 genera
Perissodactyla horses, tapirs	2 genera†	none
Rodentia giant beaver, capybaras	3 genera†	none
Reptilia giant tortoise	1 genus	none
Total	35	14 (13)‡
Percent	71 (73)‡	29 (27)‡

*Data mostly from Martin (1970) and Martin and Wright (1967).

†One or two of these genera in each order still survive elsewhere in the world.

‡ If *Euarctos* considered congeneric with *Ursus,* numbers in parentheses apply.

sheep over rabbits, although the European rabbit, like the sheep, has been domesticated and is raised commercially for meat, hides, and fur fiber. Had the Australians favored rabbits over sheep, the success of the Australian introductions would have been considered their great good fortune. It is even possible that sheep might have taken the rabbits' place as pests in the minds of Australians. It is conceivable that overgrazing by sheep has caused environmental changes favorable to rabbits, and consequently the sheep industry may be aiding its own worst enemy.

The introduction of another exotic, the rabbit disease myxomatosis from the Americas, has drastically reduced the population of Australian rabbits. When and if the resistant strain of rabbits again starts to increase rapidly, the Australians will have several possible choices. One might be to crop the rabbits heavily enough to keep down their population. Another might be to introduce new strains of myxomatosis or new diseases. Yet another might be to apply management practices to range lands that will maintain them in a relatively unfavorable condition for rabbits. The most intelligent approach may involve learning to live with a moderate abundance of rabbits.

Biotic disruptions

Both the introduction of the Indian mongoose to Hawaii and the European rabbit to Australia well illustrate how vulnerable certain biotas are to introduced species, especially when continental species are introduced to islands. The long-isolated Australian biota has been especially vulnerable to introduced species, even though Australia has an area of about 2,948,000 square miles (1,832,000 square kilometers), making it an island continent.

In Australia, as in Hawaii and some parts of the U.S.A., domestic dogs *(Canis familiaris)* have established *feral* breeding populations and live as typical wild animals. This probably does not occur in sub-Saharan Africa, although the opportunity for it has certainly existed for many years.

In North America, large and small domestic dogs were kept by the native inhabitants well before European settlement occurred, yet feral populations seem not to have been established until relatively recent times. One suspects that the elimination or near elimination of wild members of the genus *Canis* has permitted domestic races to succeed in the now vacant niches formerly occupied by wolves and coyotes.

In Hawaii, small dogs owned and eaten by native Hawaiians apparently did not establish feral populations. Both introduced sheep and large European dogs became feral. Possibly, the sheep were important as prey for them as Tomich (1969) suggests. However, the original Hawaiian dogs were small, while the dingo *(Canis dingo)* and the more recently introduced European dogs of Australia and Hawaii were quite large. It seems possible that the small Hawaiian dogs lacked more than just size, and so could not exist as feral populations even in the Hawaiian Islands.

In Africa, competition with and direct predation by living canids, felids, and hyaenids appears to be too intense to allow establishment of feral dog populations. In Hawaii and Australia, such competition was largely absent. Continental Eurasia and Africa infrequently experience population explosions among introduced species, and a resulting reduction in or loss of *endemics* (species native to a particular place). Small, isolated islands, in contrast, frequently experience such undesirable consequences from introduced species.

From this brief overview we can draw some conclusions concerning how we can handle the related problems of introductions and reintroductions of species. In many cases we can logically reintroduce species that have been locally exterminated in relatively recent times. We should be extremely cautious about introductions into small, isolated biotas, or even into relatively huge areas, such as Australia, that have been biologically isolated for long periods. We also should avoid introductions of many pathogenic organisms and of organisms likely to cause problems by displacing species that are clearly more desirable, at least at a given location.

What to do and why

In considering introductions, public attitudes must be taken into account. For example, the carp *(Cyprinus carpio)* is a valuable food fish introduced into Europe and is carefully tended and reared there by intensive pond culture methods; in the U.S.A., it is generally considered a trash fish to be locally exterminated if possible. The red deer *(Cervus elaphus)* is considered the most noble of the central European game mammals still regularly hunted. In New Zealand, where it was introduced, its extermination is strongly encouraged by official government policy. The American muskrat *(Ondatra zibethica),* the most important fur bearer in North America, has been successfully introduced into Eurasia. It is considered a nuisance in parts of eastern Europe, yet an asset to be carefully managed in the U.S.S.R. The ring-necked pheasant *(Phasianus colchicus),* introduced to the U.S.A., is considered an asset in spite of some of the agricultural damage it causes. In contrast, in New Zealand the large, wary, delicious Canada goose *(Branta canadensis),* which was introduced from North America, is regarded as a nuisance to be eliminated if possible. These races of large geese or "honkers" are the most sought-after of waterfowl now legally hunted in North America. There is no more logic in peoples' attitudes toward introductions than in their attitudes toward sporting versus commercial use of animals in the U.S.A. (page 102). One can, however, identify historical, social, and political reasons for their opinions; hence, as in political and advertising campaigns, we should be able to predict with some success what attitudes will be toward introductions of species, and roughly the amount of effort that will be required to change these viewpoints and to maintain new ones.

From a biological point of view, it is important to recognize the value of naturally impoverished biotas as "laboratories" for scientific investigations. "Island" biotas, whether isolated by water, land, or other drastically different ecological conditions, are of special importance. Adequate examples of such biotas should be carefully protected from unnatural disturbances of any type. Thus we must maintain large samples of naturally fishless lakes and of islands that naturally lack mammals. We need to make exhaustive studies of such areas to understand the intricacies of how ecosystems function. For example, by comparing fishless lakes with similar lakes naturally stocked with fish, we can hope to gain insight into the effects of fish in lake ecosystems and insight into biotic influences on evolutionary and ecological development within ecosystems.

But what of the great areas already much altered by man and his introduced domestic and wild plants and animals? In these areas what guidelines can help us make logical decisions? Assuming that public attitudes are or will become reasonably favorable, when are we justified in introducing or reintroducing a species? We are probably safe in introducing or reintroducing a species if we can guarantee that (1) the costs of introduction are not exorbitant, and (2) the introduced species can be maintained in very low abundance or be completely exterminated at reasonable ecological and monetary costs. Under these conditions we have open to us not only all the possibilities available with the species present, but also all those available in its absence. With the relatively new techniques of genetically and chemically induced sterilization (page 3), which are potentially applicable to any species, we lack only detailed techniques for control over the abundance of a particular animal species. (Because of their ability to reproduce vegetatively, many plants may be immune to these techniques.) Upon the development of such techniques, we might logically follow a suggestion of Martin (1970) that several close relatives of the former Pleistocene fauna of the southwestern U.S.A. be reintroduced to boost animal production in these arid ranges. The ability to control populations also would allow the safe introduction of endangered species into new areas to protect them from possible extinction. Lacking the ability to eliminate introduced species, it would probably be unwise to introduce them. We have had enough unfortunate experiences with such endeavors to realize that the risks taken are often unpredictable.

DANGEROUS ANIMALS—MAN AND THE GRIZZLY

Grizzly attacks

In 1967 two young women were pulled from sleeping bags, killed, and one partly eaten by a grizzly bear *(Ursus horribilis)* or bears in Glacier National Park, Montana. At other times campers were mauled or attacked but escaped by climbing trees. However, this is the only case of a grizzly eating a human in a national park, and it was attributed to a bear known to have repeatedly been fed garbage in the presence of humans. Man-eating is very rare (Herrero, 1970).

In early summer 1959, two young men were fishing along Eagle River, a short distance north of Juneau in south coastal Alaska. One carried a powerful rifle. Cutting across a bend of the river, he apparently blocked the only escape route of a brown bear (a large subspecies of the grizzly). The bear rushed the young fisherman who shot at it but missed. In charging past him to safety, the bear bit off much of his face, permanently blinding him. Public reaction was to slaughter all bears, including cubs of the much smaller black bear [*Ursus (Euarctos) americanus*]. Because of local public opinion, there was no attempt to enforce the game laws protecting such animals.

Following the Glacier Park killings, an article about it appeared in *BioScience* (Moment, 1968). The author made several points, a few of which we quote, hoping not to bias his overall meaning. "Every summer over ten million people visit parks where bears occur. . . . One comes to feel that to be critical of bears is tantamount to . . . taking a stand against motherhood. The highly dangerous character of the grizzly has been amply confirmed. . . . However, any zoologist could draw up a list of animal . . . species that we would be better off without. . . . If a species like the grizzly, which is on the endangered list, can be saved, all well and good. But there is no scientific basis for the dogmatic assertion that . . . anyone . . . is obligated to save it or any other species without regard for the human cost in money, lives, or health. . . . The morning after the fatal grizzly attacks in Glacier . . . [among] . . . the 60 or so people who had spent the night either in the chalet or in the nearby campsite . . . the reaction to the events of the previous night was virtually unanimous. The Park Service should make up its mind whether it wants to run a park for people or for bears! . . . Sober later thought indicates that it would make perfectly good ecological as well as common sense to designate certain parks, such as Yellowstone and Glacier, as areas primarily devoted to people for hiking . . . camping . . . but above all for viewing those stupendous geological sights. . . . Old Faithful is unique to Yellowstone, bears are not." Of course geysers also are not unique to Yellowstone and any particular bear living in Yellowstone is. Furthermore, most of the world's grizzlies south of the Canadian border live in these two parks.

Moment was obviously there when the killing occurred in Glacier. He was certainly shocked and horrified as anyone except the most callous would be. The incident and his reaction serve to elucidate several of the problems associated with our treatment of dangerous animals. People may suffer as a result of their continued existence. Those who do suffer and those closely associated with these people will see the extinction of dangerous animals or their banishment to far areas (suggested in Moment's article) as an effective solution, hence a desirable one. All over the world people interested in wildlife conservation are accused of not being interested in two-legged animals (mankind), only in four-legged ones. Moment apparently felt this, as shown by his suggestion that certain parks such as Yellowstone and Glacier be, ". . . areas primarily devoted to people. . . ." That is what cities are.

Status of the grizzly

In the areas administered by the National Park Service in 1969, its personnel estimated the number of grizzlies as follows: 175–225 in Glacier, 250 in Yellowstone, 6 in North Cascades, and an occasional transient through the Grand Tetons. In Alaska, Mount McKinley had about 75. In 1969 the only states allowing grizzly seasons were Alaska, with a kill of 505 from a decreasing population, and Montana with a kill of 33 (Anonymous, 1970b).

The grizzly is featured on the state flag of California. In 1924 the last known California grizzly was killed (Storer and Tevis, 1955). Today it is estimated that less than 1000 grizzlies remain in the western U.S.A. (Leopold, 1970). Wyoming grizzlies almost all occur in Yellowstone. It was thought that the last grizzly had been killed in Mexico in 1968, but there have now been reports that a few still exist (Leopold, 1970). Presumably, there are a few barren-ground grizzlies, members of a rather distinct race, roaming the vast arctic prairies of Canada. Aside from these, the last of the world's grizzlies live mostly in the mountains of western Canada and in Alaska. It was estimated that in 1969 many remained in Canada and perhaps 10,000 in Alaska (Keim, 1970). The Alaska figure includes coastal brown bears.

The former range of the grizzlies extended west to east from the Pacific coast to the Mississippi River, and northeast to the Arctic coast near Simpson Strait, Mackenzie District (Herrero, 1970), and from the Arctic Ocean south to near the Isthmus of Tehuantepec.

Human reactions to danger

How should the grizzly be treated? Or a more general, hence better, question: How should we treat the dangerous animals of the world? Which are the dangerous animals and just how dangerous are they relative to the other dangers mankind encounters and also relative to the potential benefits associated with these dangers? To simplify this discussion, we do not consider animal disease organisms or their vectors, although many of the same lines of reasoning can apply to them as well.

To begin, it will pay to consider some of the dangers we regularly face but are inclined to forget. We are delightfully frightened by tales of dangerous mammals or of dangerous diseases such as bubonic plague of man or hoof-and-mouth disease of cloven-hoofed mammals and hedgehogs. People try to frighten us about cigarette smoking with little success, and also about the dangers of riding in automobiles, again with relatively little success. Even the mortality of the Southeast Asian war is something that people seem to think will happen to someone else they never heard of. Table 6–2 gives a comparative listing of some dangers based on injury and mortality rates. It ignores the debilitating effects of sicknesses and injuries associated with many of these things. Probably among the worst of these are parasitic diseases such as malaria, filariasis, and bilharzia (schistosomiasis), and injuries from traffic accidents and warfare.

From Table 6–2 we see that we do not base our actions, at least in a very clear-cut way, on the mortality rates associated with the various dangers in our lives. This is tacit proof that as humans we use other criteria when dealing with danger. We do not necessarily avoid it; some may even seek it. Our effort must be to delineate these criteria and their variability, and to use them to achieve the best possible conservation.

Most people choose to avoid danger if they see a direct threat to themselves. If an exercise of skill or strength could allow a person to survive the danger involved unharmed, some probably would actively confront it. Why climb the sheer face of Half Dome in Yosemite? There is a trail up the other side. One might do it for money or, perhaps, publicity, but some people willingly pay considerable sums for such chances to risk their necks. Certainly, some do it for the acclaim they receive, but most seek the challenge that dangerous situations provide.

Perhaps people require contact with real or imagined danger in their lives. In the tiny town of Fayette in southwestern Wisconsin, local people still talk about a black panther (usually refers to melanistic leopards but can also refer to the cougar, *(Felis concolor)* although melanistic individuals are rare among them) in the area; and they probably still organize hunts for it. It is just barely possible that there was a black panther or a series of them in this farming area, but it is doubtful. People become bored on these farms during the winter, and if reckless driving of cars and farm

Table 6–2. Comparison of dangers*

| | Injuries | | Deaths | | |
Cause	Number	Rate per 100,000	Number	Rate per 100,000	Source
Grizzly attacks in North American national parks (all records over 97 years)	77	0.05	5	0.003	Herrero, 1970
Accidents in the U.S.A. in 1967					U.S. Bureau of the Census
All causes	44,995,000	25,520	113,169	57.2	
Rail			997	0.5	
Motor vehicle			52,924	26.7	
Aircraft			1,799	0.9	
Firearms			2,896	1.5	
Drowning			5,724	2.9	
Complications due to medical procedures			1,530	0.8	
Moving motor vehicle	2,890,000	1,640			
Therapeutic misadventure	1,368,000	780			
Injury by animal or insect	1,838,000	1,040			
Uncontrolled fire, explosion, or discharge of firearm	380,000	220			

*It should be noted that the data for grizzly attacks cover a period of 97 years, and that the rates are calculated in terms of visitors to the parks. All other rates are for 1967 only and are based on the total U.S. population, not just on those exposed to the risk. Obviously, our risk of grizzly injury is minute.

machinery is not your thing, there is always the black panther. The inhabitants of a certain area of northern California describe a huge man-ape known as Big Foot; farther north he is called Sasquatch (Green, 1968). His actual existence is about as likely as that of the black panther hunted in Wisconsin, although both are very valuable boredom dispellers for the people that reside in these areas.

Whether we make up animal dangers, ascribe excessive danger to animals such as the black rhinoceros *(Diceros bicornis)* (Fig. 6–2), or face realistic dangers from them, dangerous animals are important for man. It is important that the chance to confront dangerous animals and also the opportunity to know that it is possible to do so be preserved.

The conservation of danger

How can we preserve the opportunity to confront dangerous animals for our descendants? The presence of these animals will conflict with the

Figure 6–2. A black rhinoceros *Diceros bicornis,* in a mature mopane woodland in the Urungwe area of Rhodesia. This photo was taken with a 50 mm lens. Rhinoceros horn brings high prices as an aphrodisiac in Asia. Is it any wonder that this is an endangered species?

interests of some people. But as Herrero (1970) says regarding grizzly habitats within national parks, "Man must temporarily relinquish his role as a tamer, a reducer of wilderness, and enter into an ecosystem in which he may not be the dominant species. This can be the quintescence of man's experience in the national parks, because here man becomes a part of nature. This is the highest purpose our parks can serve."

The first necessity in order to preserve this option is public acceptance of the idea that dangerous animals are of value to mankind. The reasons for this will have to be more-or-less constantly kept before the public. When this has been accepted, the next step will be to manage the preservation of dangerous animals in such a way as to cause the least possible conflict with and danger to those that wish to be protected from them. For example, people could be warned to stay inside their cars in certain national parks, and to sleep only in buildings provided for that purpose. At the same time it seems reasonable that, completely at their own risk, they could walk either with or without a guide through areas occupied by dangerous animals and could sleep in tents or on the ground in such areas if they choose. This is somewhat new to us in the U.S.A., but it is typical in some African parks. Many seem to think that our parks ought to be kept safe enough so that the most inexperienced person can safely sleep out on the ground anywhere and anytime. In African parks this is obviously a ridiculous notion. It is also rather risky in the presence of grizzly bears.

If we are to preserve the right to enjoy the thrill of seeing wild, powerful grizzly bears, we must make it very clear that people who take risks with them do so on their own responsibility and that neither they nor their heirs can hold anyone else responsible. If this understanding is not established, the grizzly is probably doomed.

Other countries of the world often look to the U.S.A. for guidance in handling their problems. If we eliminate the grizzly from our national parks, a few countries may receive irresistible pressure to exterminate some of their dangerous animals. This could, for example, mean the end of a few endangered species such as the Asiatic lion *(Panthera leo)*. Such errors are very unlikely to occur in the better game areas of Africa, because not much of an African national park would be left if dangerous animals were eliminated. Even in our parks, it would be ridiculous to attempt elimination of poisonous snakes, and they are more dangerous than grizzlies. Hopefully, we will not be so short-sighted as to let our sympathy for victims of rogue bears lead to the extinction of the grizzly simply because we can do it. Our descendants will never forgive us.

The purpose of national parks is to preserve examples of pristine nature. In our management of the world's wildlife parks, the welfare of the natural ecosystem must take priority over our own convenience. Any other approach will certainly lead to the eventual destruction of national parks.

No one can predict the kinds of advantages that may become ours through contact with potentially dangerous animal and plant life. The poisonous plant genus *Strophanthus* produces drugs of value to mankind in the treatment of heart disease, and also produces delightfully fragrant blossoms.[1] The venom of bees has been used in medical treatment. The Norway rat, which nourishes the fleas that may carry bubonic plague, is one of the most important laboratory research mammals we have. The tsetse fly, via the trypanosomes it transmits, now prevents settlement of large parts of Africa. In so doing, it is buying us the time that could allow us to effect social and economic changes that would ensure good land husbandry when these areas are occupied. The best way to handle conservation problems is to solve them in ways that leave open the most possible

---

[1]During a field trip in Africa I picked one of these blooms and asked what it was. Our botanist claimed that a single seed of the plant I picked would be enough to poison a whole small village if it were to get into the malt for their beer.

choices. Extermination of the grizzly or any other species does the opposite.

SUGGESTED DISCUSSION MATERIAL

1. Explore local attitudes toward wildlife where you live. What apparent inconsistencies do you find? For example, are people prepared to utilize some species and not others equally abundant and secure? Do they protect females of one species but not of another with similar breeding habits? Do people who demand a stop to killing wildlife tacitly condone the killing of domestic animals by eating meat or wearing leather products? What values do people place on selected wild animals? Do their actions vary from what might be expected based upon these values? What seem to be the underlying human reasons for these inconsistencies, if any? Based upon these reasons, what courses might be followed to obtain more rational approaches to wildlife.

2. Explore the literature on game ranching in Africa and elsewhere. Discuss the possibilities of its introduction elsewhere, perhaps in your region. What problems would be encountered? What might be gained or lost? Relate your discussion to world population problems.

3. Fire and man go together. Read about and discuss the history of man's use of fire and its ecological effects. Both anthropological and ecological literature contain useful material. How has fire improved conditions for wildlife in different parts of the world? How can it be used? What disadvantages does the use of fire have?

4. What aesthetic considerations are involved in species introductions and reintroductions? Explore attitudes toward existing introductions as a means of estimating attitudes toward potential introductions.

5. How can recreational resources serve greater numbers of people as populations increase? Consider the possibilities in sport hunting, such as a return to the use of primitive weapons and restrictions on the use of mechanical transport. Are there ways to increase nonconsumptive uses that will reduce consumptive uses, and do so without doing cultural or psychological harm?

Aquatic Resources 7

PHYSICAL PROPERTIES OF WATER

Chemically pure water freezes at 0°C (32°F). As the amount of dissolved electrolyte is increased, the freezing point is lowered until, in surface seawater, freezing usually occurs at about −1.9°C (29.6°F) (Sverdrup, Johnson, and Fleming, 1942). Of all naturally occurring substances, water is the closest to being a universal solvent. Of even more importance ecologically are the facts that pure water reaches maximum density at 4 °C (39.2°F) and that it is virtually noncompressible. Its peculiar temperature–density curve guarantees that, in temperate and subarctic areas especially, there is a spring and a fall overturn of the water mass in ponds and lakes (see page 132).

OVERTURN AND PRODUCTIVITY

Spring and fall overturns recirculate nutrients that have accumulated in the bottom waters and on the surface of the sediment. In normal ecological situations this tends to increase the fertility of the surface waters advantageously. Trouble occurs when excessive nutrients enter bodies of water. In the surface layers of any body of water, chlorophyll in living plants traps sun energy to produce sugars which are stored and oxygen which is released into the water. When water is rich in fertilizing nutrients, plant growth is rapid. Unless it is as rapidly browsed, or removed in some other way, this usually short-lived plant material soon dies, and the too-familiar stinking windrows of rotting vegetation result.

Waters are often classified on the basis of their productivity. Those low in nutrients and therefore with little phytoplankton, hence very clear, are said to be *oligotrophic* (few feeding), while those rich in nutrients and phytoplankton are said to be *eutrophic* (well feeding). Disruptions in the productivity of some waters may occur, such as that caused by a high content of humic acid which colors the water brown. By reducing light penetration, this brown coloration makes the zone of photosynthesis, the *euphotic* zone, shallower than it otherwise would be. Such waters are said to be *dystrophic* (nonfeeding).

SUCCESSION

Man's acceleration of aquatic succession

The process that occurs during succession in waters is termed *eutrophication*. Except for not uncommon cases in which pollutants cause dystrophic conditions, most of the man-aggravated changes in waters result in increased eutrophication. This means that man's effects on waters are usually the opposite of his effects on terrestrial environments. On land man halts and sets back successional processes, whereas in bodies of water his usual effect is to increase the rate of succession. Natural succession in wet environments progresses toward drier conditions (see Chapter 2).

Man's activities increase the rate at which bodies of water progress toward dry-land conditions by: (1) increasing nutrients in the water through the introduction of sewage, agricultural runoff, and so on; (2) using water for industrial cooling and thereby increasing water temperature, thus elevating the rate of photosynthesis and prolonging the growing season; (3) eroding upland soils into lake, river, and ocean basins, thus fertilizing them and making them shallower; (4) diking and draining marshes; (5) channelizing and straightening streams, creating dry lands of what were formerly stream beds (but succession in the new channels is set back because water velocities are increased); (6) increasing the seasonal fluctuation in stream flow, causing side channels to dry out or even whole rivers to be dry most of the year.[1] To a small extent hydric succession is set back by man when he dredges channels in rivers, bays, and marshes; however, he usually justifies this in part by the use of the dredge spoil as a means of "reclaiming" (filling) a nearby marsh—as if man ever had any claim to it as dry land in the first place.

---

[1]One could argue with item (6). This effect of man's actions is disruptive. Although these streams are dry most of the year, they may become raging torrents during heavy rains. It is debatable whether or not successional trends can be confidently recognized in such cases.

Marsh management

In marsh management for wildlife, channels or ponds are dredged, blasted, or draglined, and small dams are constructed. Even in dry marshes that lack surface water, except during spring runoffs, ponds can be created by digging deeply below the water table. Wildlife flourishes in such areas, and the raised spoil banks provide nesting locations for waterfowl, upland gamebirds and songbirds, and denning locations for mammals. Fire is sometimes either purposely or accidently used to create open water in marshes, since the highly organic soil burns when dried out at the end of a long, dry season.[2] Burning is surely a poor method, because of the resulting air pollution and because the accumulated fertility should not be wasted. If heaped as spoil banks, the soil will grow vegetation which can protect the marsh from winds and support animal life. Wind protection slows the rate at which wave action causes a breakdown of the banks along recently opened water areas.

Dams may act either to speed or to delay hydric succession, or to do both. Damming the outlet of a marsh raises the water level, thus setting it back successionally. If the stream flow below is reduced, succession is speeded. To explain this we must digress for a moment.

Succession in lakes

During succession in a deep lake basin, materials sink to the bottom of the lake, and the ratio of water mass to surface area changes so that there is relatively more surface as time goes on. Of course, the sides of the lake also support vegetation, and this progresses toward the center of the lake as material accumulates along the shores. Here rooted aquatic plants and emergent vegetation rapidly contribute to eutrophication (Figs. 2–6, 8–1, and 8–2). Except where bogs grow across the surface (Fig. 7–1), the lake contains less and less water relative to the lake surface. This in turn provides a larger euphotic zone, relative to the amount of water. Thus as eutrophication proceeds, it normally accelerates. In general, deep lakes are oligotrophic, and shallow ones eutrophic. By damming a marsh or lake, the average water depth is usually increased, making it more oligotrophic, hence setting back succession.

---

[2]Such peat is still harvested for fuel in Ireland, and someday may again have similar value in North America.

Figure 7–1. Bog formation in Lake Aleknagik, Bristol Bay region, Alaska.
Northern pike, *Esox lucius,* and beaver, *Castor canadensis* are abundant in this
area of the lake.

Succession in flowing watercourses

The question of succession in flowing waters is not as clearly biological as
that in lakes and ponds. One tends to think more in geological terms when
it comes to rivers and streams. The braided streams of Alaska and elsewhere (Fig. 7–2) are geologically young, while the meandering streams of
the driftless (unglaciated) areas of southern Wisconsin, for example, are
geologically quite old. When man steepens the gradients of streams, he
sets back the geological succession. Likewise, a reduction in stream flow
velocities ecologically mimics what happens as streams mature. Great, flat,
tropical marshes which flow only after rains are probably examples of the
most mature flowing-water systems. These marshes apparently have existed so long that not only have certain fish become evolutionarily adapted
to them, but certain marsh ungulates have also evolved. An example of the
latter is the long-hoofed sitatunga *(Tragelaphus spekei)* of Africa.

Man's actions on flowing water depend very greatly on the situation.
Dams on streams fill more-or-less rapidly with silt. Many fill so rapidly that

Figure 7–2. A braided stream as seen from the highway between Fairbanks and Circle, Alaska. This geologically young stream supported fair numbers of Arctic grayling, *Thymallus arcticus*. Moose, *Alces alces*, frequented the surrounding riparian vegetation, and caribou, *Rangifer tarandus*, passed this area in large numbers during their migration.

the calculations of costs and benefits amortized over time have been so wrong that one finds it hard to believe that dam proponents could have been honest in their errors. Whether or not they were, the impoundments behind dams silt up just as lakes do, and this could be interpreted as increasing the rate of succession. Headwater dams, designed to discharge slowly as water levels decrease, can maintain a more constant stream flow below than that which occurred before their construction. The concept of biological succession in flowing waters is probably not very useful in understanding man's impact upon them, because geological factors seem so important in determining their history. It is very rare to find the climatic and geological stability that have allowed the formation of great seasonally flowing tropical marshes. It is true that with nutrient and heat enrichment flowing waters support fish and other animal species which in lakes are associated with more eutrophic conditions. This leads us to use water quality as a more generally useful criterion than succession when considering both flowing *(lotic)* and nonflowing *(lentic)* waters.

Lotic communities tend to undergo serial succession along their lengths. The youngest stages usually occur in the upper parts, and the more mature communities in the lower reaches. Also, the rate of change tends to be faster per mile of stream in the upper reaches than in the lower parts. This parallels secondary terrestrial succession which also shows the quickest changes during early successional stages. However, it is also regularly noted that succession is seldom continuous; instead, the life of the upper reaches may occur here and there in the lower and more slowly flowing parts of the system. In general, as the lower parts of a lotic system are reached, there are fewer rapids interspersed with pools; the stream bed becomes deeper and more uniform, and the flow more constant. In terms of their flow, the lower reaches resemble the rapids rather than the pool conditions nearer the headwaters. In the lower reaches of a mature stream system, however, the bottom tends to lack the rocks of the upstream rapids, so the *benthic* (bottom) communities are often quite different.

Lentic and lotic communities compared

In another very important way, lotic communities are quite different than lentic ones of the same region. Even in the youngest stream, the amount of shore relative to the volume and surface area of water is very large. Therefore such communities show affinities with eutrophic lakes that have nearly reached marsh pool stages (Fig. 2–6). The surrounding uplands normally have a much more important effect on what goes on in streams than on what happens in lentic communities.

At the same time, because of the presence of flowing water, lotic communities resemble the exposed and wave-washed shores of more oligotrophic lakes. Even the organisms may be very similar. When there is fairly strong wave action along the shore of a lake, the inshore waters above the thermocline (see next paragraph) are like flowing waters in that oxygen content is high and there is almost no temperature gradient. This area of a lake is also like a stream in that diurnal and seasonal temperature fluctuations are often drastic, and nutrients are distributed quite uniformly throughout the water mass.

Part of the reason why this occurs in lakes and bays is that these bodies of water tend to stratify thermally during the summer. As a result, wave action stirs only the portion above the region of rapid temperature change, hence rapid density change, the *thermocline*. With cooling of the surface layers to 4°C in the fall, the whole lake reaches this temperature and the entire mass overturns under the influence of wind. Again, the surface inshore waters continue to show little if any gradient in nutrient or oxygen concentration. With further cooling the inshore waters of a lake cool the fastest, and the formation of ice starts there.

OXYGEN DEPLETION

As nutrient enrichment increases in any body of water, an accelerated accumulation of organic detritus on the bottom occurs if the water does not move fast enough to flush it out. This detritus breaks down *aerobically* (in the presence of oxygen) at first, and then with oxygen largely exhausted, by *anaerobic* means. Consequently, oxygen depletion occurs first in the bottom sediments and finally, if the right conditions occur, the entire water mass becomes anaerobic. Needless to say, these conditions eliminate all except the air-breathing fish or those that can utilize air for oxygen through specialized gill mechanisms. There are places, mostly in the tropics, where such fish are relatively common, presumably because hot, muddy, anaerobic waters have been a common feature of the environment for a long time. Examples are the African lungfishes (*Protopterus* spp.), the walking catfishes *(Clarias batrachus)* of Asia which have been introduced perhaps too successfully into Florida, and the mudskippers (*Periophthalmus* sp.) of Australia's Queensland coastal mangrove swamps. These interesting little fish go through the same physiological changes when they dive into water that most fish do when they are taken from water (Scholander, 1963). The temperate areas of the world generally lack such highly specialized fish. The result is that severe pollution, which causes oxygen depletion, usually kills all the fish in both still and flowing temperate waters.

One of the places in which such mortality occurs frequently is in shallow lake basins that freeze over during the winter. When the snow cover occludes light from the water, photosynthesis, hence oxygen production, essentially stops. *Oxidation* and *fermentation* still occur in the sediments, and the living plants and animals of the lake continue to consume oxygen. Before long, in rich lakes, the oxygen reaches such low levels that organisms requiring oxygen-rich water succumb. Trout (*Salmo* spp. and *Salvelinus* spp.) are one of the first to go, but even small species of catfish (*Ictalurus* spp.) will be eliminated if the conditions continue too long. As is readily apparent, addition of phosphates or other nutrients into such naturally eutrophic waters aggravates the problem of winter kill, and by speeding succession we thereby lose important recreation and food resources.

SHORE EFFECTS

Lakes, bays, and rivers may experience *seiches* under the right conditions. Seiches may be caused by earthquakes, winds, changes in barometric pressure, and so on. A seiche can be easily demonstrated with a cup of tea or coffee. If the cup is rocked in just the right way, all the fluid will slosh back and forth at the same time, rising first toward the rim on one side and then toward the rim on the other. This is a seiche, and it is one reason why you should think twice before you build your dream house too close to the water of a deep lake or bay. The July 9, 1958 earthquake in southeastern Alaska shook approximately 90 million tons of rock into Lituya Bay from a maximum height of about 3000 feet. This massive rock fall created the largest wave ever known. It removed all but one tree to an altitude of 1740 feet on the bordering mountainside (Anonymous, 1958; Ulrich, 1958; Lane, 1965). This seems not to have caused a true seiche, but earthquakes do cause bodies of water to seiche, and this may occur at great distances from the epicenter. The great Alaska earthquake of March 27, 1964, caused seiches of 1.83 feet on a reservoir in Michigan, and of 1.45 feet on Lake Ouachita in Arkansas; along the Texas Gulf Coast waves as high as 6 feet were generated (Anonymous, 1968). In Alaska at the time of the earthquake the lakes were ice-covered. The waves generated by seiches there caused the ice to peel the bark off some trees along the shores. This occurred at 20 feet on Kenai Lake, and the maximum height noted was 30 feet on trees along Tonsina Lake (Anonymous, 1968). Except for the low water level of Kenai Lake at the time, waves would have come ashore 600 feet, instead of 360 feet, at Lawing (Anonymous, 1968). The potential destruction, had this been a densely settled area, can be readily imagined. Devastation along the Alaskan seacoast was considerably greater.

In spite of such hazards, seacoast, lakeshore, and river shore property bring premium prices for business, residential, and recreational purposes. The Cliff House has been a San Francisco institution for years. It undoubtedly has sold at least as much food because of its location overlooking the sea and the rocks covered with sea lions (California sea lion, *Zalophus californicus;* Northern sea lion, *Eumetopias jubata*) as it has because of its cuisine.

Water normally occupies the lowest "ground," and so everything that can be carried by water tends to move easily into bodies of water. It is easier, hence apparently less costly, to let sewage flow downhill into lakes, rivers, and oceans than it is to pump it uphill onto croplands for irrigation and fertilization purposes. Rivers have served as travel lanes for mankind for a long time. Heavy shipping is still mostly done along the world's waterways, hence cities and industries tend to be located on the shores. Water, because of its high specific heat and relatively low corrosivity, is also the ideal coolant for most industrial purposes. Once heated, it costs money to cool the water before reintroducing it into waterways, so this is seldom done in North America. Where water is more costly for industry, it pays to cool and reuse it. The rather ugly water-cooling towers associated with industry can be seen throughout Europe and Africa. These cooling towers add moisture to the atmosphere. In wet, foggy climates, this is undesirable.

OCEANS

Oceans cover nearly three-quarters of the earth, and so have an extremely important effect on weather, climate, and the chemical constituents of the atmosphere. Since oceans occupy the lowest "ground" on the earth, they serve as the ultimate sewers, receiving the natural contributions of geological erosion as well as the accidental and intentional contributions of mankind. In the past, their huge area (361.059×10^6 square kilometers) and colossal volume (1370.323×10^6 cubic kilometers) (Sverdrup, Johnson, and Fleming, 1942) have diluted the effects of human-induced changes so that, except locally, oceans superficially appear to be little changed from their original conditions of perhaps 2000 years ago. Unfortunately, there have been vast changes in oceans near the shore, and some ecologists have speculated that irreversible, deleterious changes may already have occurred throughout (Anonymous, 1970c).

The surface waters that sink to the bottom in the north polar regions of the Atlantic take approximately 800 years to flow to the Antarctic seas. There they resurface, bearing with them the nutrients they have accumulated from sediments enroute. These nutrients result in the great richness of the antarctic waters, sometimes four times greater per unit area than that of the rest of the oceans (El-Sayed, 1967). What will happen when highly persistent pollutants now being deposited in northern seas are returned to the surface many years from now? Probably no one knows, but this consideration helps to illustrate the vast temporal framework within which environmental decisions must be evaluated.

Primary production in oceans is exceedingly important not only as the base for marine food chains, but also because it contributes to the world's supply of oxygen. We need not concern ourselves with the relative merits of terrestrial versus marine plants as contributors to this oxygen supply. The loss of either would be disastrous. Many of the herbicides and insecticides applied to uplands eventually find their way into oceans. Wurster (1968) has obtained data indicating that very low concentrations of DDT reduce photosynthesis in laboratory cultures of four species of coastal and oceanic phytoplankton representing four major classes of algae. Apparently, different phytoplankton species vary in their responses to hydrocarbons, photosynthesis being inhibited more in some than in others (Menzel, Anderson, and Randtke, 1970). Thus selective toxic stress by chlorinated hydrocarbons may alter the species composition of natural phytoplankton communities, possibly favoring some species formerly suppressed by others. This may reduce biotic diversity (see page 33), and be of even greater ecological significance than loss of the primary productivity and oxygen production of more sensitive species. These findings are of a preliminary nature at present, but they certainly demand that we use caution in allowing chemicals to enter ocean waters.

TIDES

Approximately every 12.5 hours in most of the world's seas, tides complete one cycle, so that on most days the intertidal parts of ocean beaches are twice exposed and again covered by water. These tidal changes range from barely detectable rises and falls in water level to changes of as much as 50 feet (15.24 meters) or more. Smaller tides are found in the Mediterranean and on certain Pacific islands. Large tides usually occur in bays such as the Bay of Fundy and Cook Inlet, located on opposite sides of the North American continent. At any particular location it is possible to predict the time and height of low and high water. These predictions are of course approximations of the actual depth of the water that will flow over the beaches and tidal flats, because both wave action and the effects of onshore or offshore winds may significantly alter tidal effects. The reproduction of Pacific black brant *(Branta bernicla)*, a small, dark-colored goose that nests on the Yukon-Kuskokwim flats only 2 or 3 feet above the highest spring tides is sometimes threatened by unusually high water levels. Prolonged and powerful onshore winds coupled with high spring tides may raise the water level enough to flood almost all of the nests, washing away the eggs or fatally chilling them. The Arctic nesting season is so short that these birds are unable to renest. When this happens it is extremely important to protect the adult birds, so that adequate numbers will return to the nesting grounds the following year.

Where the tidal range is great, tidal currents may become very swift and powerful. When these currents meet winds blowing against them, extremely dangerous wave and current conditions may result. Many a fisherman has capsized and drowned in such waters. These tidal water movements flush estuaries, carrying with them nutrients, pollutants, phytoplankton, planktonic larvae of many marine invertebrates, and some vertebrates in juvenile stages. Small predatory fish feed in these rich waters, and are in turn fed upon by larger predatory fish, birds, seals, and so on. Many important commercial fish and shellfish are completely dependent upon intertidal areas for their existence (Hitchcock and Curtsinger, 1972). Wave and current actions carry planktonic food to sessile (attached) animals such as sea anemones, mussels, and barnacles which under natural conditions exist in great abundance in such areas. These waters, strongly influenced by tides, are thus among the most important in providing mankind with nourishment and other products of the sea. Being in close proximity to terrestrial man, they are also influenced the most by his actions.

DAMS

In most people's minds the construction of dams is seldom connected with the ecology of the sea. Yet dams may have drastic effects not only on the movements of anadromous and catadromous fishes such as salmon and true eels, respectively, but also on the geological processes in estuaries and along ocean beaches. The blocking of organic silt by the Aswan High Dam on the Nile is being blamed for the loss of nearly 18,000 tons of sardines annually in Egyptian fisheries, and ocean beach erosion is threatening the city of Alexandria. Formerly, the annual sediment contributed by the Nile provided new materials to replace those washed away from the beaches (Sterling, 1972; Farvar and Milton, 1972). As in the case of many if not most large dams, the economics of the Aswan High Dam were apparently calculated without making adequate sociological evaluations, and in ignorance of and with disregard for potential ecological repercussions. Ecologists sounded clear warnings, but as usual were not heeded.

PACIFIC SALMON FISHERIES

By blocking the reproductive migrations of fish, dams can completely eliminate them from a watershed, and so greatly reduce their abundance in the ocean. Efforts to rear salmon artificially and so mitigate the deleterious effects of dams have had some success, but other species of lesser economic value have had to fend for themselves. Because of their very considerable value as food, Pacific salmon species have been the subject of intensive study. The history of Alaskan fisheries is a typical example of the exploitation of a public resource for private profit. Packing companies built traps which completely blocked the mouths of rivers and allowed virtually no fish to ascend the streams to spawn. Many important runs were nearly eliminated in this manner. Fishermen purse-seined the mouths of streams, and even today these "creek robbers" create one of the most difficult law enforcement problems for those charged with protecting the salmon runs. A single setting of a purse seine around salmon schooled at the mouth of their home stream can yield a creek robber 20 to 30 thousand dollars worth of salmon. In the process he may nearly eliminate all spawning in a given year. This is reflected in a very poor return of adult fish 2–7 years later, depending upon the species and race involved.

SALMON BIOLOGY

Pacific salmon show a very strong tendency to return to the stream in which they were reared when their time comes to breed and die. With negligible exceptions, all Pacific salmon die after spawning. This means that these fish could be most intensively managed if the total human take occurred at the home stream. Among those races that remain in fresh water for a long time before spawning, the fish stay fat and succulent for some time after they enter fresh water. These fish could perhaps be most intensively managed within each tributary system, for we know that not only do they select the same river where they hatched but also the same tributary. In other races, especially the estuary-spawning races of pink salmon *(Oncorhynchus gorbuscha)*, the fish must be taken while they are still in the sea since, even before they enter fresh water, the fat reserves accumulated in the sea are largely consumed in the maturation of eggs and sperm and the flesh becomes lean and flavorless.

Each adult female red salmon *(Oncorhynchus nerka)* lays about 4000 eggs in a redd (nest) which she digs with her tail in a gravel stream bed. These eggs are fertilized by the male as the female extrudes them into the water. They quickly sink to the bottom and into the interstices of the gravel. The female continues to dig her redd by turning on her side and quickly flipping her tail several times. This causes the water and gravel to move upward. The gravel is then caught by the downstream current, further burying the fertilized eggs. Not long after they have spawned, the male and female salmon die, returning fertility from the ocean to their home stream.

The fertilized eggs lie in the gravel, bathed by oxygen-rich water, and there proceed through the developmental stages leading to the formation of new salmon. After the young have consumed the reserves of yolk that have nourished them through the winter while the stream is ice-locked, they swim up through the gravel. By this time the stream is usually ice-free again, and the salmon fry normally descend to a lake where they spend the next year or so (rarely three) feeding on successively larger organisms as they grow to about 3–5 inches in length (7.6–12.7 centimeters).

Usually, early the following summer these young fish lose their vertically oriented, dark-colored parr marks and become bright silver below and almost blue above, as is fitting for pelagic fish. When this happens, they start to swim toward the ocean, some of them navigating as much as 90 miles or more of lake before entering a stream leading toward the ocean. Sometimes they must pass through a whole series of lakes and streams before finally entering salt water.

Most of these downstream migrants swim to the sea during a relatively short time span, hence are also very abundant during a restricted period in the rivers near the sea. Many fish-eating animals, from arctic char *(Salvelinus alpinus)* to gulls (*Larus* spp.) to beluga *(Delphinapterus leucas),* gather in these areas to feed on them. Finally, the lucky ones reach the sea and there spend the next 1–4 years feeding voraciously, mostly on small pelagic crustaceans. Soon it becomes their turn to navigate the great stretches of the northern Pacific Ocean and ascend to their home tributary, to attain their brilliant-red nuptial color, and to spawn and die.

Fish show an interesting year-class phenomenon that is seldom, if ever, shown by animals producing relatively few long-lived offspring. Some pelagic spawning fish, such as Atlantic cod *(Gadus morhua),* produce vast numbers of eggs. If especially favorable conditions occur, resulting in high survival rates for the eggs, large numbers of fish are produced. This year-class can be traced through a fishery, where it shows up each year as an especially abundant fish in a certain fairly narrow size range. These fish of course become larger each year until all finally perish.

Year-class phenomenon and salmon management

The year-class phenomenon is also illustrated by salmon, even though the females lay far fewer eggs than do female cod. The year-class phenomenon clearly suggests that small changes in survival rate in early life history stages can have large effects on populations of adult fish. Therefore management efforts directed toward decreasing freshwater mortality could be expected to yield substantial increases in the number of adult salmon.

Let us illustrate this with a hypothetical model. We know that the average egg production in different races of red salmon ranges from 2000 to 5165 (Foerster, 1968). If we take one pair of successful spawners as a population unit, let us assume for purposes of this model that they will lay and fertilize most of 4000 eggs. If the size of the next spawning population is to remain the same as that of the parental generation, then there must be a mortality of 3998 individuals. This mortality can occur any time from the period of parental spawning through the initial spawning stages of the following generation. This model also assumes that the sex ratio of the spawners is 1:1, an assumption that appears to be only approximately correct. (Certain data show that on the average slightly more females than males actually reach the spawning grounds, but these data may in fact reflect the selectivity of the fishery.)

Table 7–1 shows the extent of actual mortality found at each of the indicated life stages of red salmon (Foerster, 1968). From this table we can see that the greatest numerical losses by far occur in fresh water. It is therefore evident that, barring substantial increased mortality at other stages, a moderate improvement in freshwater survival (as suggested by

Table 7–1. Approximate mortality rates during the life stages of a stable population of red salmon*'†

Life stage	Number at start of life stage		Percent mortality		Number lost during life stage	
Eggs and young in gravel	4000		50	(35)	2000	(1400)
Fry emergence and migration to lake	2000	(2600)	75	(60)	1500	(1560)
Lake residence	500	(1040)	92	(77)	460	(800.8)
Seaward migration and in ocean before fishery take	40	(239.2)	90		36	(215.3)
Fishery and spawning migration	4	(24)	50		2	(12)
Successful spawning	2, producing 4000 eggs, most of them fertilized (12, producing 24,000 eggs, most of them fertilized)					

*Based on Foerster (1968).

†Numbers are based on an approximate average production of 4000 eggs per spawning female. Figures in parentheses are those that would result if a 15% improvement in survival could be obtained at each of the three life history stages in fresh water before migration to sea. The assumption is made that compensatory increased mortality would not occur at later life history stages. A sixfold increase on the spawning grounds as well as in the fishery could result.

the year-class phenomenon) could result in a very large increase in returning adult salmon. For example, a 15 percent improvement in survival during the freshwater stages (Table 7–1) would cause a sixfold increase in the number of survivors that reach the fishery and the spawning grounds, provided that compensatory increased mortality does not occur during the later stages.

Considerable fluctuation in the abundance of returning salmon occurs naturally, so it is not unreasonable to think that improvement of freshwater survival should be a management goal. In fact, the success of controlled-flow spawning channels for salmon supports the soundness of this notion. In these channels nearly ideal conditions are artificially maintained for eggs. The potential for increasing egg survival in natural streams is great, and it is being intensively investigated.

Egg survival is only one aspect of maintaining adequate to optimum habitats for salmon reproduction, growth, and survival. One of the other factors amenable to human control is the number of fish taken for human use. As indicated earlier, salmon return with great fidelity to their home streams to spawn; consequently, each stream has its own stock of salmon which could be managed as a discrete unit. Any losses to a fishery that occur at sea will tend to decrease the ability to manage precisely, because an ocean fishery may accidentally remove excessive numbers of fish destined for a particular spawning area. It seems simple to manage fish within the framework of a stream or even a stream tributary, while prohibiting all take of salmon at sea except for those races that become sexually mature while still in salt or brackish water. Such management may be essential in order to obtain the maximum sustained yield. But there is reason to doubt that we will ever see management intentionally achieve a maximum sustained yield of salmon.

MAXIMUM SUSTAINED YIELD

In the management of renewable resources, the guiding principle has been to obtain the maximum sustained yield. This is probably a philosophical trap more than a valid goal of management. Pacific salmon species can serve as an example. Pacific salmon not only provide excellent eating for humans, but are also important in other respects. King salmon *(Oncorhynchus tshawytscha)* and silver salmon *(Oncorhynchus kisutch)* support large sport fisheries both on the sea and in river systems. All species are utilized for human consumption by the Indians, Eskimos, and Aleuts of western Canada and Alaska who live largely on a subsistence economy. Salmon also provide much of the food for the sled dogs making possible their way of life. Tourists and residents spend hours just watching spawning salmon. Salmon are taken commercially by fishermen using every means from sport fishing gear and gill nets to extremely efficient purse seines and salmon traps. For people living largely on a dollar economy, the salmon returning each year provide the cash that carries them through the year. Each person has his own investment in equipment and knowledge concerning his own method of fishing. The returning salmon have become a controlling influence on the life-styles of these people. What driftnetter fails to get a thrill when the corks on his net splash under as the first strong salmon of the season strikes the web? For these people many things other than pounds of salmon flesh have greater meaning. And these values are important enough that maximum sustained yield of salmon flesh will probably never be socially supported.

If we really believed in maximum sustained yield of any particular renewable resource that is consumed when used, we could not also believe in the multiple-use concept, which can be defined as the notion that more than one thing, including aesthetic rewards, can and should be produced in any one part of the globe. We would be led to growing trees as a row crop as so many foresters have done, and to raising salmon in situations so artificial that they could only be described as salmon production factories. And this has also been done. These situations, although many are forced upon us by human population and industrial growth, are a net loss to the quality of life. Unless you have joined the gulls, eagles, and bears to watch salmon spawning in a truly wild stream, you probably cannot appreciate the extent of the loss. It is certainly better to have salmon produced in a factory than no salmon at all, but what a depressing alternative!

Wise use?

Conservation has been poorly defined as wise use. This unfortunate definition and the acceptance of maximum sustained yield as a resource manager's goal have led to the formation of unfortunate rationalizations by well-meaning conservationists. These people have supported environmental uses which seriously jeopardize or eliminate aesthetic possibilities and ignore potential and actual subsidiary uses of the areas and resources in question. For example, foresters are possibly correct in stating that virgin coastal redwood forests lose about as much wood through windfall and decay as they gain through growth. They therefore cut the redwoods down as fast as is reasonably possible. They contend that this allows them to have more young trees growing in order to produce more wood per acre per year (maximum sustained yield).

Such an outlook is extremely simplistic. The term wise use to them means the utilization of timberlands for the production and harvesting of lumber and other wood products. These are certainly legitimate uses, but they are not the only ones; and in regard to virgin redwood forests, such use may be very unwise (see page 67). This example is the antithesis of a holistic approach to conservation of resources, but it is a convenient way to rationalize exploitative use of a virtually irreplaceable natural resource. Unfortunately, this kind of rationalization allows exploitative use of private as well as public resources, especially when the tax structure so often encourages it and when the owners are nonresident stockholders who demand high annual returns on their investments.

SOUTHERN SEA OTTERS, ABALONES, KELP, SEA URCHINS, AND MAN

As is true of other resources, those of the sea often are fought over by people with conflicting interests. An interestingly complex example revolves around the southern sea otter *(Enhydra lutris)* of California. At one time these otters were thought to be extinct, but they now have become locally abundant off the coast of central California. Even today they are completely protected by laws, and substantial effort is invested in enforcing this protection.

Sea otter pelts are probably one of the most valuable fur pelts in the world. Not only is the fur extremely soft, dense, glossy, and durable, but the pelts are perhaps three times the size of river otter *(Lutra canadensis)* pelts. The demand for sea otter furs resulted in their near extinction.

The sea otter is an extremely interesting mammal. Its use of a stone anvil laid upon its chest while floating is well known. It strikes its hard-shelled invertebrate prey against the anvil to expose the meat which is then eaten. Not so well known is the fact that at least some sea otters have been observed underwater and found to use stones to break abalone loose from the rocks. They also seem to have favorite stones which are cached on the bottom when they surface for air and retrieved when they dive to capture more prey (Faro, 1970). Although this is not tool making of the kind described in the chimpanzee *(Pan troglodytes)* by von Lawick-Goodall (1965), they certainly seem to have progressed beyond mere tool using.

Sea otters eat abalone, and in so doing compete directly with sport and commercial abalone fishermen. All exploit larger abalones which leave small caves and crevasses in the rocks and move out onto more exposed rock faces. The sea otter does not endanger the abalone's existence because abalones breed while they are still small and safely sheltered in rock fissures. Where abundant, however, California sea otters do seem to utilize almost all the large abalones that venture onto exposed rock faces.

But sea otters really prefer sea urchins to abalones. Sea urchins in turn eat kelp, and kelp is harvested commercially by man. Where sea otters are abundant, kelp usually is also, but sea urchins are not (Faro, 1970).

Not far distant from the sea otter habitat are offshore oil wells. If new wells are opened, some are likely to be drilled dangerously close to the present sea otter areas. Unlike seals, which possess a thick insulating blubber layer under their skins, sea otters rely on their fur to protect them from the cold waters. Sea otters quickly succumb if their fur can no longer provide insulation. They apparently spend almost their entire existence in the sea, hauling out onto the rocks or the shore less frequently than seals, sea lions, walruses, or their own northern sea otter relatives. A single large release of oil into their presently restricted habitat from an oil well accident such as occurred in the infamous Santa Barbara oil spill, or from the wrecking of a large tanker such as the *Torrey Canyon,* could conceivably exterminate the entire population.

Clearly, we can do a better conservation job for the sea otter and its world. No attempt to maximize a single resource, whether it be otters, abalone, kelp, or some other, can be justified. The optimum solution will not be easy to achieve, but it certainly will be assisted by a holistic approach that accounts for all considerations and seeks to maximize choices for the future.

INTENSIVE CULTURE OF FISH, SHELLFISH, AND OTHER AQUATIC FORMS

Historical perspective

Intensive culture of fish and shellfish has been practiced for many years in widely separated parts of the world, certainly since the Middle Ages in Europe. About A.D. 1400 laws were passed in Java to protect milkfish *(Chanos chanos)* farmers from fish thieves. Oysters *(Ostrea gigas)* have been cultured in Japan since 2000 B.C., and they were cultured by the Romans about 100 B.C. (Iversen, 1968). Fish culture in ponds was practiced before 1100 B.C. in China, and carp and four other species were cultivated in ponds together about the time of the Tang Dynasty, A.D. 618–904.

World production from fish farms has been estimated at 600,000 tons, as compared with 45 million tons produced by wild fisheries (Hickling, 1968). Such efforts are carried out in freshwater ponds, and also in ponds filled with brackish water. Many fish species have been successfully reared. At present, one of the fastest growing agriculture-type enterprises in the U.S.A. is the pond culture of channel catfish *(Ictalurus punctatus)*. By intensive management large amounts of excellent fish protein are produced per surface acre of pond. Similar methods employing herbivorous fish rather than carnivorous scavengers such as the channel catfish have been adopted in many areas. Pond culture techniques lend themselves especially well to the production of animal protein in places where such protein sources are scarce. Thus the Food and Agriculture Organization (FAO) of the United Nations expends considerable effort to assist in the development of intensive aquaculture (Schuster, Kesteven, and Collins, 1954).

Integration with agriculture

By raising ducks, pigs, or other livestock on pavement, it is possible to wash their wastes into an adjacent pond situated downhill. There the wastes encourage rapid plant growth to feed herbivorous fish. The bream (*Tilapia* spp.) of southern Africa are delicious food fish which are largely herbivorous. This places them on the same level of the food pyramid as cattle, hence they are in general more useful protein producers than freshwater predatory fish such as trout *(Salmo* spp. and *Salvelinus* spp.), sunfish (*Lepomis* spp.), and bass (*Micropterus* spp.) (see page 20).

Successful research on the pond culture of *Tilapia* in Rhodesia has involved raising ducks or pigs immediately uphill from three ponds stocked with *Tilapia*. Most of the water reaching the lower ponds seeps through earth dikes from the ponds above. Below the last pond rice is raised, and the fry stages of the *Tilapia* are reared in the water at the bases of the rice plants. Truck crops in turn are raised below the rice field. This way maximum use is made of the water. All the garden vegetables that cannot be used by humans, pigs, or ducks are thrown into the fish ponds to feed the *Tilapia*. The expertise needed to operate such a diverse agricultural venture is not readily available among peasant agriculturalists, but the potential of such enterprises has been shown to be considerable.

Recently, it has been recognized that higher protein yields result if two or more fish species with complementary food requirements are reared together (Hickling, 1968; Jackson, 1961). Recall that this technique has been successfully practiced in China since the Tang Dynasty more than 1000 years ago. There the principal fish raised together include a plant eater, a phytoplankton eater, a zooplankton eater, and a bottom feeder. Sometimes a mollusc feeder, another bottom-feeding fish, and a generalized small-organism feeder are included (Hickling, 1968). Hopefully, training programs supported by the FAO and other organizations will help in the development of this means of staving off protein starvation in some developing countries. Needless to say, pond culture is not a panacea for man's dietary protein problems, but it can help.

One of the problems in pond culture of fish is that some fish breed in the ponds. *Tilapia* do this very successfully while still quite small, and a huge population of stunted nonsalable fish soon results. Carp may also cause the same problem. Sometimes predatory fish such as trout or bass are stocked to eat the young of herbivores or fast-breeding invertebrate feeders such as sunfish. This is very commonly done in recreational fishing ponds in the U.S.A. Hickling (1968) and others have found that the crossbreeding of *Tilapia* species yields only male hybrids and that these fish grow faster than either parent. By using only the hybrids, the problem of fish breeding in ponds can be solved without resorting to the use of predatory fish.

Raising fish in sewage ponds

In the treatment of municipal sewage, wastes are usually allowed to settle and undergo anaerobic fermentation. Then the supernatant trickles through a column of coarse gravel where organisms utilize the minerals and organic matter, thus decomposing it. This process is largely oxidative, occurring in the presence of abundant oxygen. The watery material is then usually held in a series of ponds for a subsequent period, and there further biological decomposition occurs. In many cases agitators in the first of these ponds stir the water to increase oxygen content, hence oxidative decomposition is promoted.

In the second pond, fish can live very well under most circumstances. This pond is also extremely rich in nutrients, and anaerobic conditions can quickly occur should decreased photosynthesis, wave action, or a die-off of plankton take place. However, because they are so rich in nutrients, these oxidation ponds have the potential to produce rapid growth in fish. Experiments are underway in many places to develop the techniques necessary to produce fish in sewage ponds. In ponds in Munich, Germany, rainbow trout *(Salmo gairdnerii)* have been successfully reared with carp (Hickling, 1968).

At Arcata, California, federally supported studies are underway to investigate the possibility of raising salmon fingerlings for release directly into Humboldt Bay. Salmon require oxygen-rich, cold water. The cool climate of the northern coast of California assures correct temperatures, but the maintenance of correct oxygen levels may be more of a problem. At present these experiments indicate that, if all goes as anticipated, the growth of these salmon will be phenomenal. However, there will probably be many problems to solve before reliable production of salmon can be guaranteed.

Culturing shellfish and other aquatic forms

Shellfish are also cultured commercially. Along the coast of France, the culture of Atlantic mussels *(Mytilus edulis)* was started by Patrick Walton, an Irishman shipwrecked in 1235. His large net suspended on stakes driven into the tidal flat was constructed with the hope of catching birds he could eat. Instead it attracted mussel larvae that attached and grew on the web. Being an observant and resourceful person, he noticed this and refined his mussel culture system. Today the *bouchet* system of mussel culture used on the French coast is essentially that devised by a shipwrecked Irish sailor nearly 740 years ago (Ryther and Bardach, 1968).

In Humboldt Bay, where the salmon experiments described above are carried out, oysters are cultured both in beds on the bottom as well as suspended on racks where many more can be raised per unit area than is possible in the bottom beds. This technique was adopted from the Orient, and the oyster spat used are imported from Japan. One of the problems with the bottom beds is that many of them are situated on flats that formerly supported abundant stands of eelgrass *(Zostera marina)*. Humboldt Bay is a very important resting and feeding area for black brant *(Branta bernicla)* on their return migration enroute to nesting grounds on the Yukon-Kuskokwim flats in western Alaska. Eelgrass, exposed by low tides, is by far the most important food for the brant while they are in the bay. Also associated with eelgrass are many other organisms which surely suffer as a result of its loss (Waddell, 1964). Rack-cultured oysters displace less eelgrass, so in this regard rack culture seems superior to the establishment of bottom beds in the bay.

Many other aquatic organisms can be intensively cultured. These include sea squirts (ascidians), octopi, sea cucumbers, many species of fish, red and brown algae, many species of shrimp, crabs, cockles, clams, scallops, abalones, and so on (see Bardach, 1968; Bardach and Ryther, 1968; Hickling, 1968, Iversen, 1968; Ryther, 1968; Ryther and Bardach, 1968; Tamura, 1966.) It seems probable that aquaculture will increase in the future. However, Hickling (1968) gives a perceptive summary of the probable reasons why increase in its practice has been slow and probably will continue to be slow. He suggests that fish farming in developing countries might well pattern itself after that practiced in China for many centuries. In this system aquaculture is an integral part of diversified production on small, private holdings.

INTERNATIONAL CONTROL OF PELAGIC RESOURCES

Pond culture is essentially the farming of aquatic organisms. It can produce much needed protein or edible vegetable material close to dense human populations by utilizing some of their wastes and the wastes of the plants and animals associated with them. Such efforts do not by any means utilize the major production of living matter by the waters of the world. We can predict with some confidence that it will be a long time, if it ever occurs, before such intensive management is applied to the pelagic portions of the world's oceans. These waters, most of them rather abiotic, will be fished much as they are today. To assure the protection of their resources, it will be necessary to change the conditions of their use. Either through international agreements or by some other means, these resources urgently need protection from competitive exploitation. The current situation can lead only to near or total elimination of one species after another.

In effect, exploitation of the resources of the high seas follows the pattern of exploitation of a public resource for private gain, and is what Hardin (1968) terms "the tragedy of the commons." There is a slight hope that, if stabilization of both the human population and of capital occurs (see page 11), the vast size of the seas and the reduction of human pressure upon them for resources may partially solve this problem in the absence of meaningful international agreements. However, the ocean will lose far too many important resources before such stabilization can possibly be expected to occur, unless meaningful international agreements are soon effected [see Hardin (1972) for a possible solution].

PROTECTION OF WATERS

What can be done about conservation of the earth's waters? Probably one of the greatest necessities is to improve the aesthetic education of the public and to increase both legal and social pressure on those who pollute the environment.

Another approach that will have to be used in some cases is the return of materials to the source of origin or to environmentally more advantageous locations. As it is, we import large quantities of every conceivable material into areas of dense settlement, but the equally necessary export of wastes and surplus is performed in the most mindless manner. In essence we use only two methods to "rid" ourselves of those materials, gravity and fire. If it is difficult just to dump trash over a cliff, or into a marsh, lake, or river, we use water as a carrier to wash it away, with gravity providing the motive force. Burning is used either combined with these methods or alone. The results are polluted waters and trash-filled gullies and air. The disease and poisoning problems created have already reached disastrous proportions in many parts of the U.S.A. The "repatriation" of waste requires energy, hence will aggravate problems associated with energy supply, reserves, and use. However, unless this is done, there is no chance that we can eliminate or significantly reduce water pollution. This dilemma is part of the reason for the *accelerating* implosion being caused by the exponentially increasing human population and the exponentially accelerating technology of technologically advanced nations.

SUGGESTED DISCUSSION MATERIAL

1. Could aquaculture be increased in the area where you live? Would its products be able to compete successfully with aquatic products obtained from wild populations? Are there better ways to use local waters? How might the return of wild aquatic products be increased in quantity or quality? What would be the sociological implication of any action proposed?

2. Are there any controversies related to water and its use in your area? Are conservation values being given adequate consideration? Who has made previous decisions regarding water management and use in your area? What have been the legal and sociological results? Is a change needed? If so, what changes, and how can they be most smoothly carried out?

3. Explore the unique problems associated with water in arctic environments. Read about permafrost, sewage disposal, construction problems, agriculture, and related ecological processes. Relate your readings

to the special problems men face when living in Arctic environments. Discuss technological changes in Arctic life and relate these to the natural environment and especially to plants and animals, emphasizing the water relationships.

4. How can water be used to provide energy for human purposes? What is the potential for an increase in hydrological power output? How could changes in the distribution of human population and technology increase the efficiency of power obtained from water? What possibilities do you see for the use of water power on a local basis? What would the cultural and sociological effects of such a change be?

5. Compare and contrast the conservation problems associated with saltwater estuaries and freshwater marshland. What should be done to solve some of these problems? How could these actions be carried out?

The Quality of   8
Life

CONSERVATION OF HUMANITY

We have discussed the resources of the earth and have noted that much of the ability to heal man-caused scars is based on life's use of energy from the sun. Since humans are now the dominant biotic factor on earth, we must consider our own species. Although intellectually we have greater or lesser amounts of empathy for our fellow creatures, in the last analysis, without our own survival there is no hope for the continuance of this empathy or its enhancement. Our survival will ultimately hinge in large part on our *quest* for an improved existence for ourselves and our descendants. It is contended that maximum contentment and enjoyment lie deep within each person. We can utilize the philosophical energy, peace, and insight derived from our inner reservoirs to improve the lot of mankind.

The average length or quantity of our lives has increased over many years. The medical profession has had an important part in this, as have scientific researchers, sociologists, politicians, and so on. Now we must focus a larger share of our attention on improving life's quality. To do so will require that we determine the constituents of quality life, or better living. In 1928, the Republican Party called for "a chicken in every pot, a car in every garage." Although we are not sure what can guarantee quality life, we are sure that this was a very superficial aim. Of course, like most slogans, it probably was not meant to be taken literally, even though many people surely did.

Each of us is a unique creature, as can be easily proved with a little genetics and some simple mathematics. The likelihood is high, therefore, that at least the proportions and the time factors in the mix that constitutes quality life will be unique for each individual.[1] The likelihood is also high that no one will ever achieve just exactly the right mix throughout his lifetime. All the more reason to keep trying! We need to ask ourselves what *really* constitutes a satisfactory life. It had better not be based on material wealth, or we will have nearly insoluble problems ahead. It is unlikely that even the present human population could be supplied with what is now considered a good material standard of living in the U.S.A.

During Earth Week in 1970, one philosopher contended that we do not know and never will know what constitutes a quality life, but in the *effort to know* we will tend to draw closer and closer to the reality. It is a hopeful approach and, furthermore, it suits the ways of technological man. Many things we think are important to our life quality are really mechanisms utilized in an attempt to gain experiences and tangible things that are really significant. Automobiles, for example, transport us to places others hopefully will or will not go to, or they help us with the opposite sex, or they earn money for us that we use to gain the things that we think count, and so on. There are certain factors that are at least commonly experienced in a good-quality life. These include: good health; affection anticipated, realized, and given; freedom from prolonged and extreme thirst, hunger, and boredom; sexual gratification; and personal recognition. It has been stated that man's needs are security, stimulation, and identity. These are useful terms because they are so general; however, it is also profitable to become more specific. For example, where does aesthetic gratification fit in? To what extent must aesthetic gratification come in different forms, such as auditory, visual, or olfactory, or from combined uses of the senses as in music with dance? It is doubtful that anyone knows the answers to these questions, but investigative methods are being employed which can lead to a much better understanding of these factors. The change in diameter of an observers' pupil when shown photographs of different scenes is an example. A momentary increase in diameter indicates a positive reaction.

There are two very hopeful signs. First, since quality living is based on fundamental factors which need not depend upon a large annual income, it is probably well within the reach of almost everyone. This will be true if we make certain changes in the world, such as a great reduction in the mass insanity called war, and a redirection of such energies into constructive efforts to improve mankind's existence. The second hopeful sign is what appears to be the core of present thinking among young people —the desire for an end to hypocrisy. These combined with a will to conserve and improve the world for others including our descendants may well win the battle. We had better win. "Stop the world—I want to get off"

---

[1] Identical twins are a possible exception.

is only a saying. It cannot be done. Even if we had another planet to colonize, we could send only a few colonizers. The rest of us would have to stay. Our life support system is supplied by the earth and sun (Wagar, 1970).

CONSERVATION AND INDUSTRIALIZED VERSUS LESS-DEVELOPED NATIONS

Concentration of power

As suggested in the introduction (page 2), nations having surplus resources, including surplus energy, have the power to concentrate more of the world's resources under their control. Operating on the basis of apparent national best interests, nations may be expected to attempt such monopolization of resources. This is exactly the action that would be taken by any "ideal" business. If such an approach is taken, it will force more and more of the world's people into subsistence-level existence, or even into mass starvation. The factors that will especially aggravate this situation are population increases in less developed countries and increases in technological development in industrialized countries. Both processes are currently increasing exponentially.

Taking the U.S.A. as an example of an industrialized country, there is little doubt that the relatively few people who control the wealth to a large extent control the country. These people and/or their companies tend to have a powerful influence in government, so the notion of a corporate state is not far-fetched. The question then is: What brake can be applied to this concentration of power in time to avert its most serious consequences? Some of its consequences are already history.

Self-defeating pure capitalism

Fortunately, the tendency of the corporate state to function in a purely capitalistic manner is not directed solely toward other political entities but also within. Thus the continuing concentration of wealth and power in the hands of a few citizens deprives others until most people have very little of either. When the inbalance becomes sufficiently extreme, the majority has always ensured return to a more equitable distribution. This internal change also changes the external posture of the state.

One must not infer that either the largest corporations or national governments operate in a completely capitalistic manner, for to do so would very quickly bring their downfall. Also, such an inference ignores the vast amount of evidence that people both in and out of governments and corporations have struggled to assist their fellow men. The various foreign assistance programs of industrialized nations, assistance plans for their own people, industry-financed grants for education, and so on are sufficient evidence that neither national governments nor the largest corporations are completely capitalistic. However, one must also recognize that in most cases these plans are enacted because if they are not trouble will come from those needing assistance. In the case of industrially financed altruistic activities, the face value is often greater than the actual contribution because of the related tax benefits and the promotional aspects involved. The point is that the mentality involved in such social assistance is still fundamentally that of the capitalist or the realist, whichever term one prefers. At least in international dealings, this charge applies to the so-called communist countries as well as to the capitalist ones.

Fortunately this kind of "realism" will eventually be self-defeating, because people will refuse to serve it when gains appear to be considerably less than losses, and when they no longer have a moral commitment to a cause that results in their unhappiness. The dangers lie in the tendency of people, causes, and nations to maintain moral commitments far beyond a time of rational termination. Dangers also lie in the tendency of humans to see as an enemy the other team, or country, or group, or any different kind of person for that matter.

International cooperation and control

What seems necessary is a transcending effort at the international level, one that can reach beyond the boundaries of politics and geography and unite the world's people sufficiently to control the activities that otherwise will eliminate or severely jeopardize man's existence (Caldwell, 1972; Kay and Skolnikoff, 1972). Pragmatists will not expect worldwide recognition of the brotherhood of man no matter how thoroughly practical such a phenomenon would be. But they can hope and strive for enough international cooperation and control to avert catastrophe. They can be optimistic that such control will be developed because it is so clearly necessary and because any desperate country can blackmail any other on earth (see page 3). The most difficult requirement for such an attempt is the aggressor's willingness to lose everything. When there is hardly anything left to lose, such willingness becomes easier. With the accelerating concentration of power in the world, there is not much time to change the direction of international efforts. Have-not countries may soon become sufficiently desperate to take such a gamble, and it may pay off because their victims will have so much to lose.

The most powerful nations must share their affluence, hence their power, with the less powerful. They need to realize that the submission of some autonomy to international control is essential for their own existence. On a grand scale this is analogous to the necessity for governmental control within a nation. Nations never have been particularly good at solving problems that cross international boundaries. Now the important challenges to man's survival are international in character. Some control on a world basis is essential.

Strategy for nonindustrial countries

World control will probably be aimed at human population growth, at pollution, and at the use and distribution of energy and material resources. The impact of population growth is closely related to the intensity of industrialization. A very densely populated country largely dependent on peasant agriculture would suffer a major catastrophe if all families were equipped with cars and the roads and services to operate them. Its population would already be too large to allow this, yet as peasant agriculturalists, at least reasonable subsistence level would still be possible.

Energy and material resources are necessary for industrialization. Few if any of the major world powers have the material resources to support industry for long, and all now utilize the resources of countries with less technological development. Given open competition in the international marketplace, industrialized countries can and probably will continue to channel more and more of these resources toward themselves. For a less developed country to industrialize, it must also obtain resources. To do so in competition with the superpowers will become more and more difficult.

The initial stages of industrialization can perhaps be accomplished by utilizing resources lying within national boundaries. To avoid external economic pressures, manufactured products may also have to be utilized internally. The possibility of importing the same products more cheaply would have to be countered by such measures as currency controls and import duties. This may lead to internal dissatisfactions, causing political repercussions.

Industrialization like that of Germany, France, Britain, and Japan is simply not feasible for most less developed countries. Furthermore, it is probably not desired by most people in such countries. Among those that do desire it, many would change their opinions if made aware of all the implications. These people would be even more likely to change their opinions if they found that they could obtain the social and intellectual benefits of industrialization without industrializing.

Resources are essential for industrial activity. The demand for them is becoming greater and the supply less. Countries that export their resources have every reason to request and receive their fair share of the social and intellectual benefits of industrialization. If industrialized countries provide them these benefits, then they need not attempt substantial industrialization of their own. It is important that less developed countries cooperate with each other in obtaining their fair share of the social benefits that can come from the industrialization that they support.

If any one of the industrialized countries were to unilaterally provide to less developed countries the social benefits required, it would become highly vulnerable. For this reason supernational organizations are needed to plan, request, and enforce the provision of adequate and necessary social benefits for less developed nations. Conservation in all nations would improve as a result.

International planning and cooperation

The basis for such assistance lies in global classification and planning. Industrialization is most emphatically not a panacea for the problems experienced by less developed nations. Small to moderate amounts may help some countries, but each is unique and requires its own evaluation, and these evaluations change with time. Most countries will not profit from large-scale industrial development within their boundaries. Of course, some changes in the distribution and type of industrialization may well be desirable, but these changes should be ecologically sound. Until world goals are formulated, global potentials and uses classified, and global plans developed, conservation, especially in less developed countries will be thwarted. Caldwell (1972) provides a more comprehensive consideration of these institutional and economic requirements and suggests practical means toward their implementation. His suggestions merit serious consideration. [See also Kay and Skolnikoff (1972) and Harte and Socolow (1971) for important analyses of the international social and economic aspects, and Anonymous (1972) for ecological aspects.]

International cooperation on conservation issues is a national necessity, not a luxury. The growing realization of that fact should provide the impetus for its accomplishment. There is a vast amount of work ahead before adequate assistance can be given to less developed countries. The international assistance they have already received has frequently been ill-advised, as judged from our present perspective (Favar and Milton, 1972). When adequate world planning is possible, international sharing will become much more constructive. In the meantime all nations, especially less developed ones, should guard their potentials with special care. It is too easy to lose forever the keys to optimum life quality. Each group will probably have to determine its own optimum human population. This decision should be based upon scientific, objective estimates of the resources that can be drawn upon to support the population in good mental and physical health.

WHAT CAN WE DO?

Some solutions such as sharing wealth, improving waste management, and so on have already been mentioned or alluded to. These include informing oneself of the ways the earth "works" and learning to become aware of both normal and altered environments. We can even accomplish something by just pausing for a moment to appreciate the beauty and grandeur of our world. These actions provide us with the incentive to take the next steps. For these steps people of every race, nation, occupation, of all ages old enough to think about these matters, and of both sexes are needed and are essential. Successful conservation can know no boundaries. We used to say that the only boundary is earth itself, but just how much space trash is too much? How many nuclear warheads can be detonated in near space without irreversible effects leading to our end? No one knows.

Some things that should be done

It is important that we avoid setting a bad example. A good example can be set by cleaning up other's debris as well as one's own, by having no more than two children, and by waiting until one's mid-20's before having children. We can talk, write, paint, or sculpt and use the performing arts to promote good conservation. It is possible for the theatre and dance to assist effectively, much more effectively than we have seen to date. To obtain good conservation, we probably must have emotional as well as intellectual involvement. Good conservation must become a part of our ethical framework.

We can become active politically to ensure the election of candidates who will work hard for environmental and human conservation. We can also encourage such actions by writing to our elected representatives opposing bad legislation, favoring good, chastising them for "wrong" stands, and complimenting them for correct actions.

Organizations dedicated to halting world population growth need our financial support, our labor, and our expertise. The same is true of those that are attempting to reduce the deleterious impacts of technology. Remember that, even if technological problems can be solved, without a rapid end to world population growth mankind will suffer greatly. Population control is a key issue, but the other problems cannot be ignored, for if they are, untamed technology and its accompanying pollution will make our world unlivable.

We should be able to explain why the GNP is a misleading statistic and why it should have subtracted from it the GND (see page 2). We must accept that overall business growth must soon stop, because the earth's resources are finite, and probably also because minor pollution from an exponentially increasing number of industrial sources will add up to totally unacceptable major pollution no matter how hard we try to control it.

If you can develop new and better ways to halt population growth, to control the impact of technology, and to improve the quality of life, you will be performing a real service. To see that they are put into action and to obtain action on other aspects of the conservation effort, you can work either alone or join with others, as best suits your inclinations. Big achievements have already come from both approaches.

Figure 8–1. View toward Picnic Point over the University Bay marsh from near the lake drive about 1900. This area is now part of the University of Wisconsin campus at Madison. The marsh in the foreground was drained and converted first into a cornfield and then into a playing field. University of Wisconsin students obtained an agreement that a small portion, which lies out of the photograph to the left, will again become and be preserved as a marsh. This small marsh already teems with muskrats and supports very large numbers of waterfowl during migration. Compare with Fig. 8–2. (Photograph courtesy of State Historical Society of Wisconsin.)

Case history of a marsh

In Wisconson, students at the University in Madison carried a class project beyond the classroom and achieved a worthwhile conservation success. The students in Clay Schoenfeld's class on environmental resource management (McCabe and Miller, 1970) became concerned about the future of a marshy area at the west end of the campus. The area was formerly a large marsh where people speared large, spawning northern pike *(Esox lucius)* in the spring. It was diked, and drained, and maize grown in the rich soil. In recent years the tile drainage system had broken down, and part of the cornfield slowly reverted back to marsh. Trash from the university was dumped into it, and there were plans to construct lagoons. In spite of the dumping, muskrats and waterfowl made heavy use of the area. This successful conservation effort by university students can serve as an illustration of what can be accomplished. The following is a quote from their report (see Figs. 8–1 and 8–2). "By investigating the biological make-up of the marsh, and its history as well as the ecological transfiguration of the Dane County region, and surveying local sentiment about the presence of

Figure 8–2. View of Picnic Point across the University Bay marsh taken July, 1971 by Dr. H. W. Mossman. Compare with Fig. 8–1. The small marsh sponsored by University of Wisconsin students lies on the side of Willow Drive opposite which this photograph was taken.

the marsh, then reviewing the updated 'Master Plan' for the U.W. [University of Wisconsin] far west campus, the students came to the conclusion that the University's landscaping objective was not compatible with the needs and desires of the ecological and social communities of the area." They managed through the assistance of the news media to stop the illegal dumping in the marsh by the university and some of its contractors. "After some delays the CPC [Campus Planning Committee] acted on the Open Space planning proposals, including the marsh area. . . . The resolutions as approved by CPC obviously met the intent of the original student proposals. . . . The students plan to work with P&C [University's Department of Planning and Construction] to see that details worked out for establishing and maintaining the marsh area closely parallel their list of original recommendations. . . . Removal of fly ash and certain other debris from the area by the University has been completed. In addition, negotiations with the class of 1918 have indicated that the class would be amenable to the use of their 'lagoon' gift fund for establishing and maintaining the marsh area."

Their efforts were evaluated as follows. "The student team . . . took . . . two measures that gave them impetus in obtaining their objective. First, they did not draw attention . . . before having evidence to support their contentions. And when they did choose to speak out, they did so without directly implicating the University of having consciously attempted to destroy the marsh, which might have alienated those University figures who eventually were of primary consequence in saving the marsh. Second, when the students made their position known and were granted the opportunity to support that position, they offered a carefully designed plan to supplement all that they felt should and could be done in the marsh area. Without the alternate plan it is probable that their arguments would have been politely received but then forgotten. . . . The study seems to point out, however, the tendency of bureaucracies to rely almost exclusively on established procedures and organizational patterns. Thus effectual participation in bureaucratic institutional decision-making by new and/or unrepresented groups or individuals is often made difficult if not impossible. . . . Without the assistance of such strategically placed and influential individuals as the Vice Chancellor, the Director of P&C and the chairman of CPFAC [Campus Planning Faculty Advisory Committee] the students might have become discouraged in their efforts to comprehend or affect the operating system and might have abandoned their cause. Institutional receptiveness and ability to respond, whatever the official structure, still seems highly dependent on the attitudes and actions of certain well-placed individuals within that institution." The University Bay marsh was formally dedicated in mid-May 1972.

It's people who count

Not only does this case history of the University Bay marsh show what kinds of things can be accomplished, but it also goes a long way toward showing how they can be accomplished. In the final analysis it is the people involved who count. Determination and thoroughness are also key ingredients in eventually winning for conservation. If you can somehow convince key individuals to accept a conservation issue as their own personal cause, you have probably won the battle. Very few people need to be fought directly. Some irrational and dishonest tactics have unfortunately been used for conservation causes, but our strength lies in rationality and factual support. Although dishonest and irrational tactics may succeed in a few cases, they endanger the overall effort. These students have shown by design and partly by accident *how to win* honestly *for everyone.* That, in the long run, is always the result of a conservation success.

What is next? With your help we may not only be able to give our descendants a better world, but we may also be able to enjoy some of the benefits ourselves. If the satisfactions of positive action are insufficient to spur us on, the horrifying alternatives should do so.

SUGGESTED DISCUSSION MATERIAL

1. Is war necessary? What can be done to prevent or control it? Delve deeply into the place of warfare in "primitive" societies. What appear to be the biological and ecological reasons for its existence? Among people who rarely or never fought wars, and those who did, what cultural and ecological contrasts can you find? On what bases have present-day international agreements been established? War is sold. Can peace be sold? How can man's aggressiveness be turned toward the keeping of peace?

2. Does your school offer one or more courses that integrate international social, political, and conservational issues? If not, should they? If so, could you design such a curriculum? How would you work toward having it adopted?

3. Every social and racial group can lend unique insight valuable in working toward solutions of conservation issues. How do you feel in your heart about these issues? Find out how your associates feel. Do their feelings give you any insight into your own feelings? Are your deep feelings at variance with what seems rational? How do you explain these differences between rational thought and deep emotional feelings? Can you conceive of any ways to help us reconcile these differences? What are they?

4. Based on what you have learned about conservation, how do you plan to spend your life? Why? If that is looking too far ahead, have you formulated any plans for the next few years? If so, what are they and why have you chosen this way?

Glossary

abiotic • pertaining to or characterized by the absence of life or living organisms

advection • the horizontal movement of an air mass

aeolian • wind-borne

A horizon • the uppermost layer of the soil, usually rich in organic matter

albedo • (the earth's) reflectance or degree of whiteness

allopatric • originating in or occupying different geographical areas

benthic • pertaining to organisms living on the bottom of a body of water

biomass • the weight of living matter; it can be measured as wet weight or air-dried or oven-dried weight

biotic • pertaining to life

carnivore • any chiefly flesh-eating mammal of the order Carnivora

carnivorous • flesh-eating

carrying capacity • the ability of a habitat to support specific organisms over time, measured in terms of organism numbers or biomass

cercariae • larvae (usually tadpole shaped) of flukes (Trematoda). Develop from a previous stage (sporocyst or redia) in a molluscan host and are the transfer stage to the next host.

chaparral • low, dense, brush vegetation, especially of southwestern North America

clear-cutting • the felling of all standing trees

climax • the final self-perpetuating stage of ecological succession

colluvial • a means of soil formation or soils so formed; soils formed through the effects of gravity, for example, by landslides

community, biotic • the interacting organisms occupying a given area

competition • an interaction between two or more organisms, each striving at the same or different times to utilize a resource that exists in short supply such as space, food, or water

competitive exclusion • Gause's rule, or allopatry resulting from competition

conservation • the physical and/or mental utilization (such as aesthetic appreciation) of resources, in the broadest sense, that leaves open a maximum possible number and kind of alternate uses for the future

consumer • an organism that feeds on other organisms and/or their products

cyclones • low-pressure centers around which air travels; they usually have strong winds, and precipitation normally accompanies them

DDT • a fat-soluble, persistent, chlorinated hydrocarbon used as an insecticide

DDE • a breakdown product of DDT having similar characteristics and effects

decomposer • an organism that utilizes materials from dead organisms that (normally) it did not itself kill; this term is sometimes restricted to certain bacteria and fungi

disclimax • a successional stage preceding the climax that is long maintained by the action of some external force such as fire; upon removal of the external force, succession proceeds toward climax

diurnal • pertaining to the period of daylight

diversity, ecological • biotic richness; the variety within a biotic community resulting from interactions among the types and numbers of species, the numbers of individuals of each species, and their relative dominance

duff • the partly decayed vegetable matter that lies on the soil surface in forests

dystrophic • pertaining to a body of water which because of some abnormality (accumulation of humic acids, for example) supports less life than would otherwise be expected

ecocline • the biological, chemical, and physical changes along a gradient

ecology • the study of the interrelations of organisms with their environment

ecosystem • a biotic community and the environment with which it interacts; materials are cycled between the living and nonliving parts of ecosystems, while energy flows through and/or is stored within them

ecotone • a transition zone between two or more biotic communities

electrolyte • a substance that dissociates into ions when dissolved or melted and becomes a conductor of electricity. An example is table salt, NaCl, which dissociates into $Na+$ and $Cl-$ ions

emergent vegetation • plants, rooted in the bottom, that rise above the water surface

endemic • native to a particular place; not introduced

environmental resistance • a term used by Chapman to describe the summation of all extrinsic factors that restrict population increase; this term does not include intraspecific behavioral and physiological mechanisms

erosion • the natural removal of soil or other materials from their present sites; wind and water are the principal agents

erosion, gully • the movement of soil by water flowing in a channel which is deepened, widened, and made to move uphill as the erosion proceeds; rill erosion refers to the early stages of gully erosion

erosion, headwall • one aspect of rill and gully erosion which results in the channel moving uphill; water that plunges over a lip of more erosion resistant material swirls back under the lip undercutting it; this weakens the lip which breaks off; as this process continues, the gully advances uphill

erosion, rill • see gully erosion

erosion, sheet • movement of soil by water moving across it on a broad front; water velocities are usually low, but raindrop splash creates strong turbulence; humus and fine mineral particles are removed, severely reducing soil fertility

euphotic zone • the vertical zone in any body of water into which sufficient light penetrates to allow photosynthesis

eutrophic • pertaining to a lake or pond rich in nutrients, hence also rich in plant and animal life

eutrophication • a successional process in waters accompanied by increased fertility

feral • wild or untamed; usually applied to organisms that have escaped from domestication

fermentation • the release of energy by anaerobic means

fission, nuclear • the splitting of atomic nuclei to produce energy

food chain • the succession of organisms through which energy flows

food web • the interconnecting feeding relationships of organisms in ecosystems, consisting of a complex of food chains

forb • any herb that is not a grass or grasslike

fusion, nuclear • a thermonuclear reaction in which nuclei of light atoms join to form nuclei of heavier atoms, with the release of energy

game ranching • the production, under ranching conditions, of wild animals for human utilization

general adaptation syndrome • the physiological responses to stress mediated by the adrenopituitary system

glacial milk • the whitish-colored water that flows from beneath glaciers; the finely ground rock particles impart the milky appearance

green manure • green vegetation, usually nitrogen-fixing legumes, which is plowed into the soil to increase its fertility

hectare • 2.471 acres, a metric measure of area

herbivore • a plant eater

hurricane • a storm with winds of 75 miles per hour or more

hydrach • pertaining to succession on a wet site

insectivore • an insect eater

interspecific • between species

intraspecific • within species

laterization • the process that forms tropical soils called laterite; organic matter is rapidly broken down and the iron and aluminum in the soil is oxidized; lateritic soils tend to be acidic; true laterite is a mineral-rich earth which turns into a bricklike form when exposed to air; it can serve as a source of iron, and is also rich in aluminum.

lentic • pertaining to nonflowing water

loess • wind-borne soils derived from glacial scourings of rocks

lotic • pertaining to flowing water

mesic • pertaining to an environment having a balanced supply of moisture

niche, ecological • the position and/or function of an organism in an ecosystem

oligotrophic • pertaining to a lake or pond characterized by a low accumulation of nutrient salts, which supports only sparse plant and animal life and maintains a high oxygen content below the thermocline owing to the low organic content

omnivore • an organism that eats both plant and animal matter

overturn • the turning over of the water mass in a lake or pond when the water reaches maximum density throughout at 4°C

oxidation • combining with oxygen; the process releases energy

pelagic • pertaining to the open ocean near the surface and far from land

photosynthesis • the synthesis of carbohydrates, from carbon dioxide and water, using light as the source of energy and with the aid of a catalyst, chlorophyll

piscivore • a fish eater

plankton • the floating and drifting organisms in a body of water

pluvial • pertaining to rain; rainy

polygynous • pertaining to males that mate with more than one female

producer • an organism able to produce its own food from inorganic substances, usually a green plant

productivity • the rate of energy fixation via photosynthesis and/or anabolism

productivity, primary • the rate of energy fixation mostly by photosynthetic organisms

productivity, secondary • the rate of energy fixation by consumer organisms

purse seine • a net that can be drawn around the organisms to be captured and whose bottom can be closed by hauling in a line that runs through rings at the bottom of the net

pyramid, biotic • see pyramid, food

pyramid, food • a biotic pyramid; a pyramid depicting trophic levels such as producer and primary consumer

range condition • the present condition of rangeland based on its potential ability to grow vegetation useful to animals; a range in excellent condition produces maximum amounts of such vegetation, and there is no erosion in excess of normal geological erosion

range trend • the direction in which a range condition is progressing, either improving or declining

riparian • water edge

sacrifice area • an area where poor land management is (erroneously) accepted as necessary

seiche • the oscillation of the water in a lake, pond, bay or other water body caused by wind, changes in barometric pressure, earthquakes, and so on

seral community • a biotic community at some stage in the successional series between a pioneer and climax community

shock disease • a normally fatal disease that occurs when an organism is unable to mobilize glucose physiologically; often it is the terminal manifestation of the general adaptation syndrome

stability principle • the positive correlation between increasing ecological diversity and increasing community homeostasis

standing crop • the number, biomass, or some other measure of the quantity of organisms or living organic material in a specific area at a specific instant

stocking rate • the number of animals or the biomass per unit area per unit time

subnival • pertaining to beneath the snow surface

succession, biotic • the progressive replacement of one community by another in proceeding toward a climax

succession, primary • biotic succession on a bare rock or in open water

succession, secondary • biotic succession proceeding on sites influenced by life that existed there previously but which has been entirely or partly removed

swidden • an agricultural practice in the tropics; small plots in the forest are cut, and the wood stacked and burned; the ashes fertilize the crops; after 2 or 3 years of cropping, the field is abandoned and another prepared

sympatric • originating in or occupying the same geographical area

taiga • the boreal forest

territory • an exclusively occupied area or volume; in some cases it may not be stationary. An alternate definition for use in animal behavior studies is a defended area

thermocline • a region of rapid temperature change with depth in a lake, pond, or bay

tilth • the physical structure of the soil as related to its suitability for plant growth

trophic level • a position in the food chain, such as producer or primary, secondary or tertiary consumer

trypanosome • a small parasitic flagellate protozoan of the genus *Trypanosoma;* they live in blood and other body tissues and many cause serious diseases in their vertebrate hosts

utero, in • in the uterus or womb

xerarch • pertaining to succession on a dry site

References

Anonymous. 1958. Where hell breaks loose. *Alaska Sportsman,* 24(10): 6–10.

Anonymous. 1968. *The great Alaska earthquake of 1964: Hydrology.* Publication 1603. National Academy of Sciences, Washington, D.C. 441 pp.

Anonymous. 1970a. AEC Nevada site said contaminated. *The Times-Standard,* Associated Press, 23 August: 21.

Anonymous. 1970b. *Big game inventory for 1969.* Wildlife Leaflet 496. U.S. Department of the Interior, Bureau of Sport Fisheries and Wildlife, Washington, D.C. 4 pp.

Anonymous. 1970c. The talk of the town—Ocean pollution. *New Yorker Magazine,* 31 January: 28–30.

Anonymous. 1971a. Short duration grazing. *Rhodesian Farmer,* 19 February: 17–19.

Anonymous. 1971b. Treble the herd on half the acreage. *Rhodesian Farmer,* 5 February: 16–17.

Anonymous. 1971c. *Environmental quality: The second annual report of the council on environmental quality.* Superintendent of Documents, U.S. Government Printing Office, Washington, D.C. 360 pp.

Anonymous. 1972. *Man in the living environment.* University of Wisconsin Press, Madison. 288 pp.

Bannikov, A. G., L. V. Zhirnov, L. S. Lebedeva, and A. A. Fandeev. 1967. *Biology of the saiga.* Israel Program for Scientific Translations, Jerusalem. 252 pp. Originally published in Moscow in 1961.

Bardach, J. E. 1968. *The status and potential of aquaculture, par-*

ticularly fish culture. Vol. 2, Part III: *Fish Culture.* PB 177 768. Reproduced by the Clearinghouse for Federal Scientific and Technical Information, Springfield, Va.

Bardach, J. E., and J. H. Ryther. 1968. *The status and potential of aquaculture, particularly fish culture.* Vol. 2, Part I: *The status and potential of aquaculture.* PB 177 768. Reproduced by the Clearinghouse for Federal Scientific and Technical Information, Springfield, Va.

Becking, R. W. 1967. *The ecology of the coastal redwood forest and the impact of the 1964 floods upon redwood vegetation.* Final Report, National Science Foundation, January 15, 1967. Mimeo. 91 pp.

Blus, L. J., R. G. Heath, C. D. Gish, A. A. Belisle, and R. J. Prouty. 1971. Eggshell thinning in the brown pelican: Implications of DDE. *BioScience,* 21(24): 1213–1215.

Boughey, A. S. 1971. *Fundamental ecology.* Intext Educational Publishers, New York and London. 222 pp.

Buechner, H. K. 1960. The bighorn sheep in the United States: Its past, present and future. *Wildlife Monograph,* No. 4. 174 pp.

Caldwell, L. K. 1972. *In defense of earth: International protection of the biosphere.* Indiana University Press, Bloomington. 295 pp.

Calhoun, J. B. 1962. Population density and social pathology. *Scientific American,* 206 (32): 139–146.

Cantwell, R. 1970. The night the world ended. *Wisconsin State Journal,* 11 October: Section 6, pp. 1 and 3.

Carson, R. 1962. *Silent spring.* Houghton-Mifflin Co., Boston. 368 pp.

Changnon, S. A. Jr. 1972. Examples of economic losses from hail in the United States. *Journal of Applied Meterology,* 11: 1128–1137.

Chapman, R. N. 1928. The quantitative analysis of environmental factors. *Ecology,* 9(2): 111–122.

Christian, J. J. 1950. The adreno-pituitary system and population cycles in mammals. *Journal of Mammalogy,* 31(3): 247–259.

Davis, J. W., and R. C. Anderson, eds. 1971. *Parasitic diseases of wild mammals.* Iowa State University Press, Ames. 364 pp.

Dobzhansky, T. 1941. *Genetics and the origin of species.* Columbia University Press, New York. 446 pp.

Dodds, D. G. 1965. Reproduction and productivity of snowshoe hares in Newfoundland. *Journal of Wildlife Management,* 29(2): 303–315.

Ehrenfeld, D. W. 1970. *Biological conservation.* Holt, Rinehart and Winston, New York. 226 pp.

Eibl-Eibesfeldt, I. 1970. *Ethology.* Holt, Rinehart and Winston, New York. 530 pp.

El-Sayed, S. Z. 1967. *On the productivity of the southwest Atlantic Ocean and the waters west of the Antarctic Peninsula.* Antarctic Research Series, Biology of the Antarctic Seas, III. American Geophysical Union of the National Academy of Sciences—National Research Council, 11: 15–47.

Encyclopedia Brittanica. 1946. Encyclopedia Brittanica, Chicago.

Enderson, J. H., and D. D. Berger. 1970. Pesticides: Eggshell thinning and lowered production of young in prairie falcons. *BioScience,* 20(6): 355–356.

Ewig, R. H. 1972. Potential relief from extreme urban air pollution. *Journal of Applied Meteorology,* 11: 1341–1345.

Fairbridge, R. W. ed. 1966. *The encyclopedia of oceanography.* Encyclopedia of Earth Sciences Series, Vol. 1. Van Nostrand Reinhold, New York. 1021 pp.

Faro, J. 1970. *Subtidal sea otter habitat off Point Pinos, California.* Master's thesis. California State University, Humboldt, Arcata, California. 282 pp.

Farvar, M. T., and J. P. Milton. 1972. *The careless technology.* Natural History Press, Garden City, New York. 1030 pp.

Foerster, R. E. 1968. *The sockeye salmon.* Fisheries Research Board of Canada, Ottawa. 422 pp.

Geertz, C. 1963. *Agricultural involution:* The *process of ecological change in Indonesia.* University of California Press, Berkeley. 176 pp.

Giles, R. H., Jr. 1969. Wildlife management disproduct. *Wildlife Society News,* No. 120, February, p. 4.

Gillette, R. 1972. Nuclear reactor safety: At the AEC the way of the dissenter is hard. *Science,* 176: 492–498.

Gilluly, R. H. 1972. Noise: The unseen pollution. *Science News,* 101: 189–191.

Gofman, J. W., and A. R. Tamplin. 1971. *Poisoned power.* Rodale Press, Emmaus, Pa. 368 pp.

Green, J. 1968. On the track of Sasquatch. John Green, Box 152, Harrison Hot Springs, B.C., Canada. 78 pp.

Green, R. G., and C. L. Larson. 1938. Shock disease and the snowshoe hare cycle. *Science,* 87: 298–299.

Grosvenor, M. B., and M. Severy, eds. 1958. *Man's best friend.* R. R. Donnelley and Sons Co., Chicago. 432 pp.

Guggisberg, C. A. W. 1963. *Simba*. Chilton Books, Philadelphia. 309 pp.

Guthrie, R. D. 1972. Re-creating a vanished world. *National Geographic,* 141(3): 294–301.

Hardin, G. 1968. The tragedy of the commons. *Science,* 162: 1243–1248.

Hardin, G. 1972. Exploited seas—An opportunity for peace. *BioScience,* 22(12): 693.

Harte, J., and R. H. Socolow, eds. 1971. *Patient earth.* Holt, Rinehart and Winston, New York. 364 pp.

Herrero, S. 1970. Human injury inflicted by grizzly bears. *Science,* 170: 593–598.

Hickel, W. J. 1971. *Who owns America?* Prentice-Hall, Englewood Cliffs, N.J. 299 pp.

Hickey, J. J., ed. 1969. *Peregrine falcon populations: Their biology and decline.* University of Wisconsin Press, Madison. 596 pp.

Hickling, C. F. 1968. *The farming of fish.* Pergamon Press, Oxford. 88 pp.

Hinton, H. E., and A. M. S. Dunn. 1967. *Mongooses: Their natural history and behaviour.* University of California Press, Berkeley. 144 pp.

Hitchcock, S. W., and W. R. Curtsinger. 1972. Can we save our salt marshes? *National Geographic,* 141(6): 729–765.

Hoffer, E. 1951. *The true believer.* Harper and Row, New York. 176 pp.

Honegger, R. E. 1968. *Red data book.* Vol. 3: *Amphibia and Reptilia.* International Union for Conservation of Nature and Natural Resources, Morges, Switzerland. Loose leaf.

Iltis, H. H. 1970. *Corn and cows are not enough! The uses of diversity.* First National Congress on Optimum Population and Environment, Chicago. Mimeo. 13 pp.

Iversen, E. S. 1968. *Farming the edge of the sea.* Garden City Press, Letchworth. Hertfordshire, England. 301 pp.

Jackson, P. B. N. 1961. *The fishes of Northern Rhodesia.* Government Printer, Lusaka. 140 pp.

Kay, D. A., and E. B. Skolnikoff, eds. 1972. *World eco-crisis: International organizations in response.* University of Wisconsin Press, Madison. 324 pp.

Keim, C. J. 1970. Saving the *Ursus horribilis. American Rifleman,* 118(11): 22–25.

Krantz, G. S. 1970. Human activities and megafaunal extinctions. *American Science,* 58(2): 164–170.

Krull, W. H. 1969. *Notes in veterinary parasitology.* University Press of Kansas, Lawrence. 599 pp. Loose leaf.

Lack, D. 1947. *Darwin's finches.* Cambridge University Press, Oxford. 208 pp.

Lane, F. W. 1965. *The elements rage.* Chilton Books, Philadelphia. 346 pp.

Leopold, A. 1933. *Game management.* Charles Scribner's Sons, New York. 481 pp.

Leopold, A. 1949. *A sand county almanac.* Oxford University Press, New York. 226 pp.

Leopold, A. S. 1970. Weaning grizzly bears. *Natural History,* 79(1): 94–101.

Lorenz, K. 1966. *On aggression.* Harcourt Brace Jovanovich, New York. 306 pp.

Lowenthal, D. 1968. Environmental perception project. *Man and His Environment* (Newsletter of The Committee for the Experimental Study of Populations), 1(5): 3–6.

McCabe, R., and B. Miller. 1970. *The University Bay marsh: a case study.* Mimeo. 20 pp. Available from the Center for Environmental Communications and Education Studies, 602 State Street, University of Wisconsin, Madison.

McHarg, I. L. 1969. *Design with nature.* Natural History Press, Garden City, N.Y. 197 pp.

Martin, P. 1970. Pleistocene niches for alien animals. *BioScience,* 20(4): 218–221.

Martin, P. S., and H. E. Wright, Jr. 1967. *Pleistocene extinctions: The search for a cause.* Yale University Press, New Haven. 453 pp.

Maxwell, G. 1967. *Seals of the world.* Constable and Co., London. 151 pp.

Meadows, D. H., D. L. Meadows, J. Randers, and W. W. Behrens, III. 1972. *The limits to growth.* A Potomac Associates Book, Universe Books, New York. 205 pp.

Melville, R. 1970. *Red data book.* Vol. 5: *Angiospermae.* International Union for Conservation of Nature and Natural Resources, Morges, Switzerland. Loose-leaf.

Menzel, D. W., J. Anderson, and A. Randtke. 1970. Marine phytoplankton vary in their response to chlorinated hydrocarbons. *Science,* 167: 1724–1726.

Meyer, B. S., and D. B. Anderson. 1939. Plant physiology. Van Nostrand Reinhold, New York. 696 pp.

Moment, G. B. 1968. Bears: The need for a new sanity in wildlife conservation. *BioScience,* 18: 1105–1108.

Moncrief, L. W. 1970. The cultural basis for our environmental crisis. *Science,* 170: 508–512.

Mossman, A. S. 1966. Wildlife and the tsetse fly in Rhodesia. *National Parks Magazine,* 40 (228): 10–15.

Myers, N. 1972a. The long African day. Macmillan Co., New York. 404 pp.

Myers, N. 1972b. National parks in savannah Africa. *Science,* 178: 1255–1263.

Namias, J. 1972. Influence of northern hemisphere general circulation on drought in Northeast Brazil. *Tellus (Sweden),* 24(4): 336–343. From *Physics Abstracts,* December 1972.

Outcalt, S. I. 1972. A reconnaissance experiment in mapping and modeling the effect of land use on urban thermal regimes. *Journal of Applied Meteorology,* 11: 1369–1373.

Paddock. W. C. 1970. How green is the green revolution. *BioScience,* 20(16): 897–902.

Payne, W. J., W. J. Wiebe, and R. R. Christian. 1970. Assays in biodegradibility essential to unrestricted usage of organic compounds. *BioScience,* 20(15): 862–865.

Rappaport, R. A. 1967. *Pigs for the ancestors.* Yale University Press, New Haven and London. 311 pp.

Reich, C. A. 1970. *The greening of America.* Random House. Bantam Books edition published in 1971. 433 pp.

Riehl, H. 1972. *Introduction to the atmosphere.* 2nd ed. McGraw-Hill Book Co., New York. 516 pp.

Roos, D. v. d. S. 1972. A giant hailstone from Kansas in free fall. *Journal of Applied Meteorology,* 11: 1008–1011.

Rudd, R. L., and R. E. Genelly. 1956. *Pesticides: Their use and toxicity in relation to wildlife.* California Department of Fish and Game, Game Bulletin No. 7, 209 pp.

Ryther, J. H. 1968. *The status and potential of aquaculture, particularly invertebrate and algae culture.* Vol. I, Part II: *Invertebrate and algae culture.* PB 177 767. Reproduced by the Clearinghouse for Federal Scientific and Technical Information, Springfield, Va.

Ryther J. H., and J. E. Bardach. 1968. *The status and potential of aquaculture, particularly invertebrate and algae culture.* Vol. I, Part I:

The Status and potential of aquaculture. PB 177 767. Reproduced by the Clearinghouse for Federal Scientific and Technical Information, Springfield, Va.

Scholander, P. F. 1963. The master switch of life. *Scientific American,* 209(6): 92–106.

Schuster, W. H., G. L. Kesteven, and G. E. P. Collins. 1954. *Fish farming and inland fishery management in rural economy.* FAO Fisheries Study No. 3. FAO, Rome. 64 pp.

Scotter, G. W. 1971. Fire, vegetation, soil and barren-ground caribou relations in northern Canada. *In* Slaughter, C. W., R. J. Barney, and G. M. Hansen, eds. *Fire in the northern environment—A symposium.* Pacific Northwest Forest and Range Experiment Station, Portland, Oregon, pp. 209–230.

Selye, H. 1956. *The stress of life.* McGraw-Hill Book Co., New York. 324 pp.

Sibley, C. G. 1950. Species formation in the red-eyed towhees of Mexico. *University of California Publications in Zoology, Berkeley,* 50(2): 109–194.

Simon, N. 1966. *Red data book.* Vol. 1: *Mammalia.* International Union for Conservation of Nature and Natural Resources, Morges, Switzerland. Loose leaf.

Stebbins, G. L., Jr. 1950. *Variation and evolution in plants.* Columbia University Press, New York. 643 pp.

Stebbins, R. C. 1949. Speciation in salamanders of the plethodontid genus *Ensatina. University of California Publications in Zoology, Berkeley,* 49(6): 377–526.

Sterling, C. 1972. Superdams: The perils of progress. *The Atlantic Monthly,* 229(6): 35–41.

Storer, T. I., and L. P. Tevis. 1955. *California grizzly.* University of California Press, Berkeley, California. 335 pp.

Sverdrup, H. U., M. W. Johnson, and R. H. Fleming. 1942. *The oceans.* Prentice-Hall, Englewood Cliffs, N.J. 1087 pp.

Talbot, L. M. 1970. Endangered species. *BioScience,* 20(6): 331.

Tamura, T. 1966. *Marine aquaculture.* Translation from the revised 2nd Ed. Charles E. Tuttle Company, Rutland, Vt. Reproduced by National Technical Information Service, Springfield, Va.

Taubenfeld, H. J., and R. F. Taubenfeld. 1972. Forecast for tomorrow: Legal storm over who owns clouds. *Los Angeles Times,* 26 November: Section F.

Teer, J. G., J. W. Thomas, and E. A. Walker. 1965. Ecology and management of white-tailed deer in the Llano Basin of Texas. *Wildlife Monograph* No. 14. 62 pp.

Tomich, P. Q. 1969. *Mammals in Hawaii: A synopsis and notational bibliography.* Bernice P. Bishop Museum Special Publication 57, Bishop Museum Press, Honolulu. 238 pp.

Trewartha, G. T. 1968. *An introduction to climate.* McGraw-Hill Book Co., New York. 408 pp.

Ulrich, H. 1958. Night of terror. *Alaska Sportsman,* 24(10): 11, 42–44.

U.S. Bureau of the Census. 1970. *Statistical Abstract of the United States.* 91st ed. Washington, D.C.

U.S. Bureau of Sport Fisheries and Wildlife. 1970. *Big game inventory for 1969.* Wildlife Leaflet 492. Washington, D.C.

Vincent, J. 1966. *Red data book.* Vol. 2: *Aves.* International Union for Conservation of Nature and Natural Resources, Morges, Switzerland. Loose leaf.

von Lawick-Goodall, J. 1965. New discoveries among Africa's chimpanzees. *National Geographic,* 128(6): 802–831.

Waddell, J. E. 1964. *The effect of oyster culture on eelgrass (Zostera marina L.) growth.* Master's thesis, California State University, Humboldt, Arcata, California, 48 pp.

Wagar, J. A. 1970. Growth versus quality of life. *Science,* 168: 1179–1184.

Watt, K. E. F. 1968. *Ecology and resource management.* McGraw-Hill Book Co., New York. 450 pp.

Webster's New World Dictionary. 1970. 2nd college ed. World Publishing Co., New York.

Weinberg, A. M. 1971. Prudence and technology. *BioScience,* 21(7): 333–335, 338.

Weisman, M. N., L. Mann, and B. W. Barker. 1965. *Camping: An approach to releasing human potential in chronic mental patients.* 121st Annual Meeting of the American Psychiatric Association. Mimeo. 9 pp.

Wells, R. W. 1968. *Fire at Peshtigo.* Prentice-Hall, Englewood Cliffs, N.J. 243 pp.

White, H. E. 1948. *Modern college physics.* VanNostrand Reinhold, New York. 776 pp.

Woodwell, G. M., P. P. Craig, and H. A. Johnson. 1971. DDT in the biosphere: Where does it go? *Science,* 174: 1101–1107.

Wurster, C. F. 1968. DDT reduces photosynthesis by phytoplankton. *Science,* 159: 1474–1475.

Wynne-Edwards, V. C. 1964. Population control in animals. *Scientific American,* 211(2): 68–74.

Supplementary
Readings

Although listed by chapter, many of these sources have materials relevant to two or more chapters.

CHAPTER 1

Allison, A., ed. 1970. *Population control.* Penguin Books, Harmondsworth, Middlesex, England. 240 pp.

Detwyler, T. R., ed. 1971. *Man's impact on environment.* McGraw-Hill Book Co., New York. 731 pp.

Hardin, G., ed. ca. 1964. *Population, evolution and birth control.* W. H. Freeman and Co., San Francisco. 341 pp.

Love, G. A., and R. M. Love. 1970. *Ecological crisis: Readings for survival.* Harcourt Brace Jovanovich, New York. 342 pp.

Lundberg, F. 1968. *The rich and the super-rich.* Bantam Books, New York. 1009 pp.

Thomas, W. L., ed. 1956. *Man's role in changing the face of the earth.* University of Chicago Press, Chicago. 1193 pp.

Vayda, A. P., ed. 1969. *Environment and cultural behavior: Ecological studies in cultural anthropology.* Natural History Press, Garden City, New York. 485 pp.

CHAPTER 2

Connell, J. H., D. B. Mertz, and W. W. Murdoch, eds. 1970. *Readings in ecology and ecological genetics.* Harper and Row, New York. 397 pp.

Darlington, P. J., Jr. 1957. *Zoogeography: The geographical distribution of animals.* John Wiley and Sons, New York, 675 pp.

Hazen, W. E., ed. 1970. *Readings in population and community ecology.* 2nd ed. W. B. Saunders Co., Philadelphia. 421 pp.

Kormondy, E. J., ed. 1965. *Readings in ecology.* Prentice-Hall, Englewood Cliffs, N.J. 219 pp.

Kormondy, Edward J. 1969. *Concepts of ecology.* Prentice-Hall, Englewood Cliffs, N.J. 209 pp.

Macfadyen, A. 1963. *Animal ecology: Aims and methods.* Isaac Pitman and Sons, London. 344 pp.

Odum, E. P. 1971. *Fundamentals of ecology.* 3rd ed. W. B. Saunders, Philadelphia. 574 pp.

Phillipson, J. 1966. *Ecological energetics.* St. Martin's Press, New York. 57 pp.

Wiens, J. A., ed. 1972. *Ecosystem structure and function.* Oregon State University Press, Corvallis. 176 pp.

Wilson, E. O., and W. H. Bossert. 1971. *A primer of population biology.* Sinauer Associates, Stamford, Conn. 192 pp.

CHAPTER 3

Anonymous. 1965. *Soil erosion by water: Some measures for its control on cultivated lands.* FAO Agricultural Development Paper No. 81. FAO, Rome. 284 pp.

Bennett, H. H. 1955. *Elements of soil conservation.* McGraw-Hill Book Co., New York. 358 pp.

Brainerd, J. W. 1971. *Nature study for conservation: A handbook for environmental education.* Macmillan Co., New York. 352 pp.

Cook, R. L. 1962. *Soil management for conservation and production.* John Wiley and Sons, New York. 527 pp.

Jacks, G. V., and R. O. Whyte. 1939. *Vanishing lands; a world survey of soil erosion.* Doubleday, Doran and Co., New York. 332 pp.

Osborn, F. 1948. *Our plundered planet.* Little, Brown and Co., Boston. 217 pp.

Owen, O. S. 1971. *Natural resource conservation: An ecological approach.* Macmillan Co., New York. 593 pp.

Shepard, W. 1945. *Food or famine, the challenge of erosion.* Macmillan Co., New York. 225 pp.

Stallings, J. H. 1957. *Soil use and improvement.* Prentice-Hall, Englewood Cliffs, N.J. 403 pp.

Steffernd, A., ed. 1957. *Soil: The yearbook of agriculture 1957.* 85th Congress, 1st Session, House Document No. 30. Superintendent of Documents, Washington 25, D.C. 784 pp.

CHAPTER 4

Darling, F. F., and J. P. Milton, eds. 1966. *Future environments of North America.* Natural History Press, Garden City, New York. 767 pp.

Dasmann, R. F. 1965. *The destruction of California.* Macmillan Co., New York. 247 pp.

Dasmann, R. F. 1971. *No further retreat: The fight to save Florida.* Macmillan Co., New York. 244 pp.

Dasmann, R. F. 1972. *Environmental conservation.* 3rd ed. John Wiley and Sons, New York. 473 pp.

DeBell, G., ed. 1970. *The environmental handbook.* Ballantine Books, New York. 367 pp.

Dorst, J. 1970. *Before nature dies.* Translated by Constance D. Sherman. Houghton Mifflin Co., Boston. 352 pp.

Holdren, J. P., and P. R. Ehrlich, eds. 1971. *Global ecology: Readings toward a rational strategy for man.* Harcourt Brace Jovanovich, New York. 295 pp.

Segerberg, O., Jr. 1971. *Where have all the flowers, fishes, birds, trees, water, and air gone?* David McKay Co., New York. 303 pp.

Smith, G.-H., ed. 1971. *Conservation of natural resources* 4th ed. John Wiley and Sons, New York. 685 pp.

CHAPTER 5

Anonymous. 1964. *Weather and man; the role of meteorology in economic development.* WMO Publication No. 143, TP. 67. World Meteorological Organization, Geneva. 80 pp.

Atkinson, B. W. 1969. *The weather business: Observation, analysis, forecasting and modification.* Doubleday, Doran and Co., Garden City, New York. 192 pp.

Brown, T. L. 1971. *Energy and the environment.* Charles E. Merrill Publishing Co., Columbus, Ohio. 141 pp.

Cox, G. W., ed. 1969. *Readings in conservation ecology.* Appleton-Century-Crofts, New York. 595 pp.

Longley, R. W. 1970. *Elements of meteorology.* John Wiley and Sons, New York. 317 pp.

Lowry, W. P. 1968. *Weather and life: An introduction to biometeorology.* Oregon State University Book Stores, Corvallis.

Massachusetts Institute of Technology. 1970. *Man's impact on the global environment: Assessment and recommendations for action.* MIT Press, Cambridge, Mass. 319 pp.

Massachusetts Institute of Technology. 1971. *Inadvertent climate modification.* MIT Press, Cambridge, Mass. 308 pp.

National Academy of Sciences—National Research Council. 1966. *Weather and climate modification problems and prospects.* Publication No. 1350. Washington, D.C. Vol. 1, 28 pp; Vol. 2, 198 pp.

National Science Foundation. 1968. *Human dimensions of the atmosphere.* U.S. Government Printing Office, Washington, D.C. 174 pp.

Sewell, W. R. D., ed. 1966. *Human dimensions of weather modification.* Department of Geography Research Paper No. 105, University of Chicago. University of Chicago Press, Chicago. 423 pp.

Shapley, H., ed. 1953. *Climatic change: Evidence, causes, and effects.* Harvard University Press, Cambridge, Mass. 318 pp.

Taubenfeld, H. J., ed. 1970. *Controlling the weather: A study of law and regulatory procedures.* Dunellen Co., New York. 275 pp.

CHAPTER 6

Allen, D. 1962. *Our wildlife legacy.* Rev. ed. Funk and Wagnalls, New York. 422 pp.

Anonymous, 1969. *Wildlife habitat improvement handbook.* Forest Service Handbook FSH 2609.11. U.S. Department of Agriculture Forest Service. U.S. Government Printing Office.

Brown, F. A., J. W. Hastings, and J. D. Palmer. 1970. *The biological clock: Two views.* Academic Press, New York. 94 pp.

Darling, F. F. 1960. Wild life in an African territory. Oxford University Press, London. 160 pp.

Dasmann, R. F. 1964. *African game ranching.* Macmillan Co., New York. 75 pp.

Dasmann, R. F. 1964. *Wildlife biology.* John Wiley and Sons, New York. 231 pp.

Gilbert, D. L. 1971. *Natural resources and public relations.* Wildlife Society, Washington, D.C. 320 pp.

Giles, Robert H. ed. 1969. *Wildlife management techniques.* 3rd ed. revised. Wildlife Society, Washington, D.C. 623 pp.

Golley, F. B., and H. K. Buechner, eds. 1968. *A practical guide to the study of the productivity of large herbivores.* IBP Handbook No. 7, Blackwell Scientific Publications, Oxford. 308 pp.

Hart, W. J. 1966. *A systems approach to park planning.* IUCN Publications New Series: Supplementary Paper No. 4. International Union for the Conservation of Nature and Natural Resources, Morges, Switzerland. 118 pp.

Luce, G. G. 1971. *Biological rhythms in human and animal physiology.* Dover Publications, New York. 183 pp. Originally published in 1970 as *Biological Rhythms in Psychiatry and Medicine.* Public Health Service Publication No. 2088.

National Academy of Sciences. 1970. *Land use and wildlife resources.* Printing and Publishing Office, 2101 Constitution Avenue, Washington, D.C. 262 pp.

Teague, R. D., ed. 1971. *A manual of wildlife conservation.* Wildlife Society, Washington, D.C. 206 pp.

CHAPTER 7

Bennett, G. W. 1971. *Management of lakes and ponds.* 2nd ed. Van Nostrand Reinhold, New York. 375 pp.

Lagler, K. F. 1956. *Freshwater fishery biology.* 2nd ed. William C. Brown Co. Dubuque, Iowa. 421 pp.

Oglesby, R. T., C. A. Carlson, and J. A. McCann, eds. 1972. *River ecology and man.* Academic Press, New York. 465 pp.

Ricker, W. E., ed. 1968. *Methods for assessment of fish production in fresh waters.* IBP Handbook No. 3, Blackwell Scientific Publications, Oxford. 313 pp.

Ricketts, E. F., and J. Calvin. 1962. *Between Pacific tides.* 3rd ed. Revised by J. W. Hedgpeth. Stanford University Press, Stanford, California. 516 pp.

Tilton School Water Pollution Program. 1971. *A curriculum activities guide to water pollution and environmental studies.* Vols. 1 and 2. Training Grants Branch, Water Quality Office, Environmental Protection Agency, Washington, D.C.

Wagner, R. H. 1971. *Environment and man.* W. W. Norton and Co., New York. 491 pp.

Warren, C. E. 1971. *Biology and water pollution control.* W. B. Saunders Co., Philadelphia. 434 pp.

Welch, P. S. 1948. *Limnological methods.* McGraw-Hill Book Co., New York. 381 pp.

CHAPTER 8

Benarde, Melvin A. 1970. *Our precarious habitat.* W. W. Norton and Co., New York. 362 pp.

Black, A. 1971. *A new radical's guide to economic reality.* Holt Rinehart and Winston, New York. 114 pp.

Dolan, E. G. 1971. *Tanstaafl: The economic strategy for environmental crisis.* Holt, Rinehart and Winston, New York. 115 pp.

Ehrlich, P. R. 1968. *The population bomb.* Ballantine Books, New York. 223 pp.

Esser, A. H., ed. 1971. *Behavior and environment: The use of space by animals and men.* Plenum Press, New York. 411 pp.

Glass, D. C., and J. E. Singer. 1972. Behavioral after-effects of unpredictable and uncontrollable aversive effects. *American Scientist,* 60(4): 457–465.

Helfrich, H. W., Jr., ed. 1970. *The environmental crisis.* Yale University Press, New Haven. 187 pp.

Ogden, S. R., ed. 1969. *America the vanishing: Rural life and the price of progress.* Stephen Greene Press, Brattleboro, Vermont. 242 pp.

Index

A

Aardwolf (*Proteles cristatus*), 22

Acacias (*Acacia* spp.), 34, 61; *A. albida*, 62

Adaptation: to cold, 31, 34; to fluctuating natural conditions, 31; to heat, 31, 34

Adrenal cortex, 39

Aerobic (oxidative) decomposition, 133, 145

Aesthetic impoverishment, 100

Africa, 6, 7, 38, 63, 64, 65, 80, 112

Aggressive behavior, intraspecific, 33

Agriculture: chitemene, 72-73, 75; cut and burn, 72-73, 75; grape growing, 45-46; paddy rice, 73; peasant, 74-76; peasant and mechanized compared, 70-71; swidden, 72-73, 75; unuseable areas for, 65

A.I.D. (U.S. Agency for International Development), 7

Aid programs, 7

Air pollution, 92, 93, 129

Alaska, 6, 47-49; salmon fisheries in, 137

Albedo, 93-95; aircraft condensation trails and, 93; clouds and, 94; earth energy balance and, 93-94; inadvertent increase of, 95; polar ice and, 94; smog and, 94

Allen's rule, 34

Allopatry, 33

Alternatives. *See* Options

Anaerobic decomposition, 133, 145

Andesite, 47

Animal feeding: effects of, 61-62; signs of, 63; time factors and intensity, 62-64

Animal movements, 49-50, 63

Antarctic, 37

Anthropologists, social, 7

Antibiotics released by plants, 32

Antler growth, 25-26

Ants, 21

Aquaculture: assisted by Food and Agriculture Organization, 144; history of, 144; integration with agriculture, 144-145; many organisms cultured, 147; multiple species pond culture, 144, 145; in sewage ponds, 145-146; of shellfish, 146-147

Arctic, 37, 119

Arctic Ocean, 119

Ascidians, 147

Asia, 80

Atom bomb, 15

Atomic Energy Commission (AEC), 15

Auk, great (*Penquinus impennis*), 100

Australia, 115

Authority figure, 39

Autocratic government, 10

Avalanche, 42

B

Badger, American (*Taxidea taxus*), 102

Bangladesh, 90

Bass (*Micropterus* spp.), 23, 144

BaTonga, 76

Bay of Fundy, 136

Bear, black (*Ursus americanus*), 102-103, 118

Bear, grizzly (*Ursus horribilis*), 106, 118-124; attacks on humans, 118-119; barren-ground race, 119; in Canada, 119; coastal brown bears, 118,